C000185107

# BUSES

## YEARBOOK 2021

Edited by STEWART J. BROWN

# BUSES
## YEARBOOK 2021

FRONT COVER: *An ADL Enviro400 MMC operated by Stagecoach London is seen in Beckenham High Street on its way to Elmers End, shadowing the Tramlink route.* PETER ROWLANDS

PREVIOUS PAGE: *Against the backdrop of the imposing Lloyd's Bank building a First Optare Solo SR arrives back at Market Jew Street, the main street in Penzance town centre, on service A17 which runs from Pendeen to St Ives.* JOHN YOUNG

BACK COVER (UPPER): *A Midland Classic Optare Metrocity shows the brighter livery used for the Airline 9 service to East Midland Airport, launched in 2019. However, in this summer 2020 view the bus lacks route branding because the route had been temporarily withdrawn as a response to the coronavirus pandemic.* CLIFF BEETON

BACK COVER (LOWER): *Lothian Buses shook off its conservative and traditional madder and white livery in 1999 with what became known as the harlequin scheme, seen here on a Wright-bodied Volvo B7RLE in Princes Street in 2010.* SJB

Published by
**Key Publishing Ltd**
**www.keypublishing.com**

ISBN: 978 1 913295 66 0

Printed in Malta by **Melita Press**
Paola. Pla 3000
Malta. Europe

All rights reserved. No part of this book may be reproduced or transmitted in any form or by any means, electronic or mechanical, including photocopying, recording or by any information storage and retrieval system without permission from the publisher in writing.

© Key Publishing Ltd 2020

**www.keybuses.com**

*In the 1990s, First became one of Wrightbus' most important customers. Buses of this style could be seen from Aberdeen in the north to Cornwall in the south, as First chose Wrightbus as its main body supplier. This Scania L94UB with Wright Axcess Floline body was new to First Glasgow in 2000.* SJB

# The rise, fall and Ryse of Wrightbus

*Sir William Wright in 2016.*

**Buses** magazine editor **Alan Millar** follows the story of the UK's second largest bus manufacturer from small but ambitious origins through success, failure, and rescue in new ownership.

ABOVE: *A high spot in the Wrightbus story was winning the contract to design and build 1,000 New Routemasters for London between 2011 and 2017. This is an early example, operating for Metroline in Victoria Street.* ALAN MILLAR

Wrightbus — the UK's second biggest bus builder and the only one left in British ownership — is the stuff of legends. A family firm that in 70 years grew from modest beginnings in a Northern Ireland town into a volume manufacturer with global clients and vehicles in all major UK fleets.

It is a story of many successes, but also some setbacks, culminating in its rescue from administration in autumn 2019. It is still in family ownership and remains based in Ballymena, Co Antrim. Only there has been a change of family.

This story about buses is also about people. Those who made it a success for most of its first 73 years and key customers whose loyalty rewarded this ambitious newcomer with many repeat orders.

Above all, it is about William Wright, who was 19 when his father founded the business in 1946 as Robert Wright Coachworks and crowned a

distinguished career by being knighted in 2018. Also Jack Kernohan who joined the company as a teenager in 1955 and became its sales director, design director Trevor Erskine who created many of its products over the 25 years that it established itself as a serious builder of buses, and Mark Nodder who led the company through 20 years of expansion into a builder of complete vehicles.

William Wright, Jack Kernohan and Trevor Erskine — natives of Co Antrim — from the mid-1970s were ambassadors for a company unknown beyond the six counties of Northern Ireland.

They forged relationships with chassis and component suppliers, found out what operators expected of a bus body and how they might win their business. They impressed outsiders with their willingness to listen and learn, and for the charm with which they convinced them to deal with a business in a part of the UK that had been blighted by civil disorder and paramilitary activity since 1969 and separated from them by a stretch of sea.

What by then was Robert Wright & Son had started as a vehicle repairer. Its founder was a skilled joiner and it was with timber that the company began building commercial vehicle bodywork, turning later to metal. It met a wide range of requirements in Northern Ireland, including complex vehicles like mobile shops and libraries, van- and truck-derived school buses.

Wright's also built small coaches for the home-grown showbands that were popular across Ireland into the early 1970s, playing to large audiences in dance halls and village halls in a pre-disco age.

It wanted to build 'proper' buses too, but that market was impenetrable. The state-owned Ulster Transport Authority, with a monopoly outside Belfast, assembled its own bodywork. Belfast Corporation had its buses bodied by Harkness Coachworks off the city's Shankill Road, later by MH Coachworks, which in turn became Potters.

The landscape changed when the UTA's bus, train and road freight businesses were separated from January 1967 and given a commercial focus that, for the new Ulsterbus company, put an end to bodybuilding. Wright's lacked the experience to fulfil the new state company's needs, but displayed no shortage of ambition, and by 1969 was bidding for orders for single- and double-deck bodies.

It lost out to Alexander's, which acquired the Potters business, but Wright's dogged persistence brought the first of many Ulsterbus orders in 1982.

The break-up of the UTA had already led to the first order for public service buses. The Northern Ireland government had hived off two groups of routes to private operators and one of them, Sureline Coaches in Lurgan, Co Armagh, turned to Wright's for two new 11m single-deckers in 1973.

These were front-engined Ford R1114s with two-door bodywork on frames supplied by Seddon's Pennine Coachcraft business in Oldham and built to Pennine's design, but the front radiator grille had a prominent W in its centre, an early iteration of a trademark feature of Wright's buses today.

### The Man with the Designs

While William Wright and Jack Kernohan had been with the company man and boy, Trevor Erskine brought a wider perspective when he joined in 1976 aged 41. This talented automotive designer returned home from England, where he had worked latterly for the Ford Motor Company on the Fiesta car and Cargo truck and began changing how Wright's designed and manufactured its products.

*One of the two Wright-bodied Ford R1114s built for Sureline Coaches in 1973 to a Pennine Coachcraft design.*
REG LUDGATE

Seeking transformative ideas that might give the company a competitive advantage, he and his two senior colleagues travelled regularly to the major European bus and truck exhibitions. Contacts established on one such visit led, in 1978, to Wright's becoming the first UK licensee of the Swiss company Alusuisse's M5438 bolted aluminium system — a robust, precise, corrosion-free lightweight body structure that was easy to repair.

Now it had the technology and the talent to bid for orders from across the Irish Sea. Trevor Erskine cloaked Wright's bodies with understated designs that were distinctive yet practical, achieving aerodynamic profiles with flat rather than expensive curved glass.

The first order from Ulsterbus for two Leyland Leopards followed this formula and Wright's won bigger orders for school and social services buses in Scotland and England, supplying over 150 alone to Strathclyde Regional Council.

That led to an early setback, the ultimately unsuccessful establishment in 1981 of a satellite factory in Scotland. Wright Jenkins, later Wrights of Wishaw and then Wrights Coachworks (Scotland) was moved within Lanarkshire from Wishaw to Bellshill but closed by 1992.

Wright's broke into the mainland UK market for public service buses and coaches in 1982. It had a potentially promising chassis partner in Bedford, still a significant force among independent operators. One municipal undertaking, Maidstone Borough Council, had replaced its double-deckers with Bedford single-deckers and in 1982 bought seven plus a demonstrator with the Wright TT body.

In partnership with the General Motors styling team, Wright's developed the stylish Contour coach that Bedford hoped would make its lightweight chassis hold their own against a rapid move to competitors' heavy-duty chassis. This combined the structure of the TT with bonded glazing, a raked and curved windscreen, and semi-concealed rear wheels. Its front profile anticipated market leader Plaxton's Excalibur unveiled nine years later.

Bedford entered the project in 1982 apparently committed to buying at least 50, but the Contour was more expensive than competitors' products and demand for its coaches was falling away. It only took 30 before General Motors quit the UK bus and truck market. Wright's built six others, three on Leyland Tiger chassis, a Ford R1015, an Albion Equipment Company Puma and a Volvo B10M, the last Contour produced in 1987.

*A Contour-bodied Bedford YNT bought by Michaels of Carshalton, south London in 1984.* JOHN ALDRIDGE

*Two Handybus-bodied Dennis Darts operating with CentreWest when it was a London Buses subsidiary.* ALAN MILLAR

As with the Scottish factory, the Contour cost the company money and struck caution into Wright's, which gave up on coaches and was wary of pursuing other futuristic designs. However, the B10M was the first step in a partnership with Volvo that resumed in the mid-1990s, grew exponentially, and endured for another quarter century.

## New Opportunities

The upheavals in the mid-1980s presented Wright's with a chance to move nearer to centre stage. Deregulation, privatisation, route tendering in London, the end of new bus grants, the dismemberment of British Leyland and the closure of MCW changed the types of buses that operators required, how they bought them and from whom.

Although it missed out on the first large-scale purchasing of minibuses, Wright's was ready for the second wave, developing its TS body, later named NimBus, on Mercedes-Benz and Renault Dodge light truck chassis, selling it to such customers as Ulsterbus, Dublin Bus and Western Travel, a buyout of part of the National Bus Company.

Its sales effort went beyond taking orders. It sold on quality rather than price and it sold a unique company culture. The Wright family are

*Buyers of the 'Classic' style of low-floor single-decker included National Express Group's bus operations in the West Midlands and Dundee. This Volvo B10L with the Liberator body was delivered to Travel Dundee in 1997.* ALAN MILLAR

Presbyterian Christians who do not drink alcohol, work on Sundays, or allow the company to work on Sundays. They sought long-term relationships with customers and employees.

Relationships established from the late 1980s paid off when key contacts and organisations grew in influence and importance. Among them was Peter Hendy, a product of London Transport's graduate management training programme, who became Transport for London's commissioner, equivalent of its chief executive, and a knight of the realm.

He was in his early 30s when he first encountered Wright's in 1987, leading a project to introduce high-frequency minibuses. Trevor Erskine came up with a design based on Leyland's mid-engined Swift. The order went elsewhere, for the Mercedes-Benz 811D with Alexander Sprint body, but the superior structure and ease of repair of the NimBus led to an order for 90 from CentreWest, a new London Buses subsidiary led by Peter Hendy.

They were delivered in 1990 and London Buses bought a further 37 NimBus bodies. No one could know it then, but the seed sown by that order grew into TfL commissioning 1,000 bespoke New Routemaster double-deckers over 20 years later.

Fire wrecked the town centre factory in November 1989 before the first London vehicles were delivered, but this was the opportunity for expansion, as Wright's moved into a former textile factory on the Galgorm Industrial Estate in Ballymena, premises it expanded several times over the next 25 years.

Wright's would specialise henceforth in building buses for the UK, Ireland and international markets.

It would develop larger single-deckers, expand its sales, marketing, and aftersales efforts.

The first new product, launched in autumn 1990, was the Handybus on the rear-engined Dennis Dart. This epitomised Trevor Erskine's ultra-lean approach to design; it was highly practical, well proportioned, easy to repair but in no way flamboyant.

Essentially it was a rectangular box, with either a flat single-piece or split windscreen or, as built in quantity for London Buses, a two-piece screen with the driver's glass angled to reduce reflections, just like Leyland's recently introduced Lynx, which echoed single-deckers of 40 years earlier. Just over 400 were built, including four for Stevensons of Uttoxeter on Leyland Swift chassis.

## The Classic is Born

Next were single-deckers of up to 12m on heavy-duty chassis, for which operators expected curved front mouldings and windscreens. Known retrospectively and informally as the Classic range, these were given names determined largely by which chassis a body graced.

They began in 1992 with 25 Endeavour express coaches for Ulsterbus Goldline routes, built on Volvo-engined Leyland Tigers, the last Leylands that Wright's bodied and the only vehicles of this style with mid rather than rear engines.

Next was the Endurance, of which over 450 were built. There were 10 were on Scania K93CRB chassis for Yorkshire Traction, and nearly 300 on the Volvo B10B for customers that included West Midlands Travel, Merseybus, West Riding, Blazefield and GM

Buses North. There also were 26 Scania N113CRBs and 38 on two Mercedes-Benz chassis, the O405 and OH1416. Mercedes-Benz branded the O405 in Britain as the Cityranger and supplied it with its own front end; it called the OH1416 the Urbanranger.

The Scanias and 21 of the 22 O405s went to another future knight of the realm and figure of growing influence who rewarded Wright's with big volumes of repeat business.

Moir Lockhead — an engineer — was chairman of GRT Bus Group, the privatised Grampian undertaking in Aberdeen that was acquiring other public sector fleets and investing in high-specification vehicles with double-glazing and air conditioning. GRT merged with Badgerline in 1995 to become FirstBus, later FirstGroup, with the future Sir Moir as its chief executive.

He had first encountered Wright's in the 1980s when Jack Kernohan had tried to sell him a Contour coach. He liked the people and products and made Wright's the group's main bodybuilder.

*An Eclipse Fusion-bodied Volvo B7LA bendybus with First West of England on a service to the University of Bath.*
ALAN MILLAR

*An Eclipse Gemini-bodied Volvo B7TL, new to Go-Ahead London and cascaded to Thames Travel by 2018.* ALAN MILLAR

## Low-floor Pioneer

Important as these orders and products were, it was Wright's pioneering development of low-floor buses that set it apart.

William Wright had been following developments in Europe, where German manufacturers introduced low-floor busees in the 1980s, and was convinced that UK politicians would heed disability campaigners' call for accessible public transport.

With London Transport and the Department for Transport keen to introduce low-floor buses, he expressed Wright's early interest, tried and failed to persuade Volvo to be its chassis partner and worked instead with an initially reluctant Dennis, which developed a low-floor version of its Cummins-powered Lance.

London Buses required 68 two-door single-deckers and Go-Ahead Northern five with a single entrance/exit for a trial on Tyneside. Wright's won the orders for all 73 and developed its Pathfinder body, externally like the Endurance but with additional strength for a step-free floor ahead of the rear axle.

The London order was split between two chassis builders. Dennis supplied 38 and Scania 30 of its low-floor N113CRL. Go-Ahead also bought Lances, and orders followed for another 22, of which 10 were funded by Essex County Council.

There might have been more, but the rapid development of so many new models caused Wright's to fall behind with deliveries. Mercedes-Benz fulfilled further orders for the step-entrance O405 (including more from GRT) with bodywork by Optare, which also held an Alusuisse licence.

Dennis declined to wait when further orders were placed for the low-floor Lance and, much to Wright's chagrin, had 40 bodied by Berkhof in the Netherlands. So ended what Wright's had hoped would be a lasting partnership between two UK firms. That was perhaps an impossible dream, as Dennis had prospered by offering its chassis to most bodybuilders rather than exclusively to one.

Undaunted, Wright's developed other partnerships and built over 3,300 low-floor bodies to this style on a variety of chassis.

These were the Axcess-ultralow on the Scania L113CRL and Axcess Floline on its L94UB successor, the Crusader on Volvo's B6LE rival for the Dennis Dart (and on over 150 low-floor Darts after the companies made up their differences), Crusader 2 on the wider B6BLE that replaced it, Liberator on Volvo's B10L, Renown on B10BLE and Fusion on 40 articulated B10LAs for First.

*One of First's StreetCar-bodied Volvo B7LAs in Swansea.* ALAN MILLAR

Floline was Wright's registered name for a clever structural change that removed the need for bonded glazing and ramped the floor to reduce the number of steps into the rear. Besides the Scania, it was incorporated into the Renown and later Crusaders. It made over 850 Renowns and around 600 Scanias.

Final additions to this range were the Cadet in 2000 on the DAF SB120, a Dart-specification vehicle that Arriva (the DAF importer for the UK) persuaded the Dutch manufacturer to build primarily for its own fleets, and the Commander in 2001 on the larger SB200. Both models lived on after DAF Bus became VDL Bus, and some Cadets were sold without manufacturers' badges as the Merit, supplied by Volvo after it discontinued the B6BLE in 2002. Wright's built nearly 1,000 of the DAF/VDL models.

## New Names, New Models

The company restructured itself in 2000. Robert Wright & Son became the Wright Group (later Wrights Group to differentiate it from an unrelated company in another market), with three operating subsidiaries then and more added later.

Wrightbus would manufacture vehicles and sell them in the UK and Ireland, Customcare would provide aftermarket support, and Expotech would develop exports. Wright's had already built 25 Crusader-bodied Dennis Darts for Canberra, the Australian capital, in 1997. While the names changed, the products were still badged as Wright.

Figuring more prominently in the organisation was Mark Nodder, a Blackpool-born lawyer who joined Wright's in 1998 with initial responsibility for exports and aftersales. He became group managing director in 2006 as William Wright's son, Jeff, stepped back from operational management. He proved adept at driving the business forward while meeting the expectations of the owning family.

Wrightbus had new models to sell. Wright's had come to the October 1999 Coach & Bus show with its Millennium range, a new look for the introduction of Euro3 emission standards, and names inspired by a solar eclipse witnessed on August 11 that year.

The new body on the Scania L94UB (and its K230UB successor in 2007) was the Solar, while its Volvo equivalent — initially on the B7L with nearside rear engine — was the Eclipse. Their articulated versions were Solar Fusion and Eclipse Fusion. The naming theme was evolved in 2007 with the Meridian on 28 MAN NL273Fs and Pulsar on over 600 VDL SB200s. It was built around Aluminique, a structural system that Wright's developed when the licensing arrangement with Alusuisse expired after 20 years.

Characterised by a single-piece windscreen in the shape of a letter D rolled over by 90°, and an arched ceiling inside, it incorporated many details to simplify maintenance. Trevor Erskine gave the show exhibits — a Scania and Volvo for First — semi-enclosed rear wheels, like the Contour coach. Production vehicles had conventionally open wheels.

Production of the Eclipse Fusion began in 2000, with the 12m Eclipse and Solar following in early 2001. Twenty years on, over 4,000 Millennium bodies have been built, more than 2,500 on Volvo chassis, mainly the B7RLE with centre rear engine, introduced from 2003. The body on this simpler chassis was named Eclipse Urban (the B7L body became Eclipse Metro but few more were built), then Eclipse 2 after a styling update in 2009 and Eclipse 3 on the Euro6-engined B8RLE introduced in 2015.

The high-floor Eclipse Commuter, which Trevor Erskine conceived in semi-retirement, was unveiled in 2004. Also built on the B7RLE, this was an interurban vehicle with an extended low front overhang to accommodate a wheelchair and two of its 51 seats. Wrightbus only built four: two demonstrators and two for Stagecoach, as Dumfries & Galloway Council favoured it for improvements it was funding on a cross-country route. Yorkshire Coastliner ordered six but changed to the Eclipse Urban, which could accommodate buggies.

It also built 221 high-floor Eclipse school buses for Ulsterbus in 2007-10, on the standard B7R coach chassis and equipped with a side wheelchair lift. Those funded from the Northern Ireland education budget were called Eclipse SchoolRun; the others were known as High Capacity.

Production of the Solar ended in 2011, with over 800 built including a multi-purpose Solar Rural variant for Ulsterbus, produced from 2008.

## Gemini, StreetCar and complete vehicles

A double-decker was finally added to the range in 2001. The Eclipse Gemini on Volvo's B7TL chassis (Euro4 B9TL from 2007 and hybrid B5LH from 2009) retained the look of the new single-deckers, complementing the deep driver's windscreen with a mirror image top deck counterpart. The restyled Eclipse Gemini 2 followed in 2009.

Most of the first two years' production was for London, but orders also came from major fleets across England, Scotland and Ireland. Having a double-decker also helped Wrightbus achieve more export sales, winning orders on the tri-axle Volvo B9TL from Hong Kong and Singapore.

It built over 7,000 Eclipse Gemini and Eclipse Gemini 2 on Volvo chassis by 2017. Arriva's continued relationship with DAF/VDL brought around 200 of the Pulsar Gemini from 2003 to 2006, on the Dutch builder's DB250 chassis, mainly for London.

Wright-bodied Volvos formed the bulk of First's new vehicle purchases and in September 2004 Moir Lockhead revealed artist's impressions of the StreetCar, a Wright-bodied B7LA bendybus designed to look like a tram and deliver rapid transit for an affordable price. Design engineer Paul Blair, recruited in 1997 as Trevor Erskine's successor, developed this eye-catching creation, with front wheels moved forward, beneath a raised driver's cab separated from the passenger saloon. Its raked front was more like an express train, and the high ceiling created the ambience of a modern tram.

A prototype was ready by March 2005 and 39 were introduced in York, Leeds, and Swansea between 2006 and 2009 on routes branded 'ftr' (text shorthand for 'future'). All have been replaced by conventional buses, but Wrightbus exported 50 others to Las Vegas in 2008-09 on its own design of hybrid chassis.

A joint venture with United States chassis builder Chance Coach (later called Optima Bus) lasted from 2000 to 2009, with a version of the Millennium body built in Wichita, Kansas on a locally built chassis.

The Las Vegas contract marked the beginning of Wrightbus's transformation from a bodybuilder into

*Wright-designed bodywork on an American-built Optima Opus in Miami.* ALAN MILLAR

*A StreetLite Max in the First Manchester fleet.* ALAN MILLAR

a manufacturer of complete vehicles, which for the UK started with the Gemini 2DL integral double-decker in 2009.

This incorporated Cummins-powered chassis modules supplied by VDL, which the Dutch manufacturer called the DB300 although the vehicles were registered as Wrightbus products. Over 450 were built by 2013, almost exclusively for Arriva fleets in London and, in lowheight form, other parts of England and Wales.

With First's Sir Moir Lockhead demanding lighter vehicles, Wrightbus launched the StreetLite single-decker in 2010, powered then by a Cummins engine, more recently by a Euro6 Mercedes-Benz engine in a collaboration agreement that saw Wrightbus involved briefly in a manufacturing venture in India.

The StreetLite came in two forms, the WF wheel forward layout like the Optare Solo and the larger DF door forward, which was subsequently extended into the 11.5m StreetLite Max with up to 45 seats. First bought around 700 of the DF and Max versions, out of over 1,700 StreetLites built by 2020, but Wrightbus's share of the group's orders has diminished since Sir Moir retired in 2011. A left-hand-drive StreetLite WF was built for VDL, which badged it as the Citea MLE and sold 11 in the Netherlands and Denmark.

Wrightbus worked with its other long-standing ally, Peter Hendy, and colleagues at Transport for London on its highest profile project of all, the three-door, twin-staircase New Routemaster that was a symbol of Boris Johnson's tenure as mayor of London.

A TfL competition to design and build a new hybrid double-decker narrowed down to Wrightbus and Alexander Dennis. Despite having less chassis-building experience, Wrightbus won the contract at Christmas 2009 partly on the strength of its Aluminique structure, partly also because Peter Hendy judged that it was more likely to build the vehicle that TfL wanted. TfL hired architect Thomas Heatherwick to work with Wrightbus on its design.

One thousand were built between 2011 and 2017, all with Cummins engines, giving Wrightbus a guaranteed share of the London market. It increased production at Ballymena and established a new chassis-building subsidiary, En-Drive, initially in premises 15miles away in Antrim.

It launched the StreetDeck double-decker in 2014 with Euro6 Mercedes-Benz engine (later also in mild hybrid form as the StreetDeck HEV96). This was offered alongside but in competition with Volvo's new B5TL diesel and B5LH hybrid launched in 2013. Volvo had no lightweight single-decker like the StreetLite, but the StreetDeck — and the partnership with Daimler — changed the dynamics of its 20-year relationship with Wrightbus.

Paul Blair redesigned the double-deck body, which on Volvo chassis became the Gemini 3. Like the New Routemaster, its top deck windows are shallow. The first vehicles (including early StreetDecks) retained the Gemini 2 front — as have all those built for Dublin Bus — but it was restyled in 2014, gaining a sharp-edged look nicknamed 'Stealth' (after the American bomber) that drew on car styling. This was adapted later for the Eclipse 3 single-decker.

With the New Routemaster contract and Boris Johnson's time as mayor of London ending, its body was adapted as an alternative to the Gemini 3 on the B5LH chassis, principally for London. This was the

SRM, standing apparently for Son of Routemaster. Only eight were built, as new mayor Sadiq Khan distanced himself from his predecessor's symbols.

Volvo also distanced itself from Wrightbus, sourcing bodies for London and elsewhere from MCV in Egypt and working with Alexander Dennis on the triaxle B8L specified by Lothian Buses, which ended its lengthy association with the products of Ballymena. Volvo also has lost ground in the UK bus market.

## A perfect storm

A perfect storm was blowing into Wrightbus. Demand for new vehicles was declining and the market in London was open again to all.

There also were problems of the company's making: build quality and reliability issues, especially with StreetLites and StreetDecks; it was moving into a big new factory complex in Ballymena that was hard to fill; and the Wright family's laudable but arguably misguided commitment to its workforce had led it to build buses for Hong Kong in Ballymena instead of Malaysia at the lower price already agreed.

Fast running out of cash and with no successor appointed for Mark Nodder, who retired in March 2019, the company went into administration that September with the immediate loss of all but around 50 jobs.

*Reading Buses bought six StreetDecks in 2016 with glazed staircase panels, an optional feature on the StreetDeck and Gemini 3 that first appeared on the New Routemaster.* ALAN MILLAR

Rescue came a month later when industrialist Jo Bamford, from the family that owns the JCB construction equipment company, bought Wrightbus and imported some JCB expertise, including new chief executive Buta Atwal.

Jo Bamford's interest in bus building stems from his Ryse Hydrogen business, which produces hydrogen for vehicles and other applications. It already was in a consortium with Wrightbus to build zero-emission hydrogen fuel-cell buses. He wants Wrightbus to lead the large-scale adoption of hydrogen fuel-cells in buses, while also building battery electric and diesel vehicles.

That builds on the achievements of Sir William Wright, 92 when the company collapsed and still pursuing ideas for new technology. He predicted in the 1990s that air quality would follow disability accessibility as a policy objective for governments, and developed battery electric, hybrid, and hydrogen fuel-cell vehicles.

Wright's was in a Futurbus consortium in the 1990s, along with FirstGroup, promoting a diesel fuel-cell. It failed to take off, but Wrightbus built eight hydrogen fuel-cell single-deckers, based on the Pulsar 2-bodied VDL SB200, between 2010 and 2013 for a trial in London that ended early in 2020.

Before the collapse, it developed the StreetDeck FCEV (Fuel Cell Electric Vehicle), the world's first hydrogen double-decker, and has taken orders for 38 in the UK. Jo Bamford hopes that is the start of something big that will inject new life into a business that has been around since 1946.

# England's Southwest

A week's holiday in July 2019 provided **John Young** with the ideal opportunity to rediscover Devon and Cornwall. And the excellent weather aided his attempts to catch up on transport developments in this beautifully scenic part of the UK.

LEFT: *One of the oldest buses encountered was this veteran X-registered First Mini Pointer Dart, almost 20 years old but wearing its age lightly. It is arriving at Taunton's Tower Street bus station. It was new to First Bristol in 2000.*

MIDDLE: *A baker's dozen of these unusual Caetano-bodied MAN 18.270 gas buses joined the Plymouth CityBus fleet from fellow Go Ahead Group operator Anglian Buses. Vehicle number 711, new in 2013, traverses the city centre*

BELOW: *One of a fleet of 26 Stagecoach ADL Enviro400 MMCs for core service 12 in Torbay is seen here at Livermead, heading for Brixham, with the town of Torquay evident behind. All but five of the 26 carry this red livery.*

ALL IMAGES BY THE AUTHOR

ABOVE: *Park-and-ride livery is carried by this Stagecoach ADL Enviro200 MMC seen in Plymouth city centre. Five of these buses were delivered to Stagecoach South West in 2016, three of which are in this livery.*

LEFT: *Derriford Hospital is to the north of Plymouth. A Plymouth CityBus Yellow Flash-liveried ADL Enviro400 takes on passengers on service 51, bound for the city centre.*

BELOW: *All ten Volvo B7RLEs in the Plymouth CityBus fleet moved north to Go North West's Manchester operation in late 2019. This bus is seen in Liskeard on the service from Padstow to Plymouth via Wadebridge and Bodmin. The full journey takes two hours and 45 minutes.*

ABOVE: *The well-established operation of Wright's of Polperro, trading as the Polperro Tram Company, uses converted Crompton Electricar milk floats to link Crumplehorn car park at the top of the town through the narrow streets down to Polperro harbour. The oldest member of the fleet, Maud, is seen here at the lower terminus.*

LEFT: *A First Kernow short ADL Enviro200 is seen at the Fowey, Safe Harbour Hotel, terminus. Space is at a premium here, with drivers having to perform a tricky reversing manoeuvre. The bus will return to Mevagissey via Par, St Blazey, Charlestown and St Austell.*

*Also at Fowey, approaching the terminus, is one of First's ADL Enviro200 MMCs used regularly on the route. The green Kernow livery contrasts with the old-style corporate First colours on the bus in the previous photograph.*

ABOVE: *The cross-city park-and-ride service in Truro is operated by First with a fleet of blue-liveried Mercedes Benz Citaros.*

BELOW: *A First Dennis Trident/Plaxton President passes through Carnon Downs as it works a morning journey on service 231 between Truro and Penwith College. First operates a large network from most parts of Cornwall to cater for the college's transport needs. This bus was new to CentreWest in 2002.*

*Routes U1 and U2 link Falmouth and the Penryn Campus of the University of Exeter with Truro (U1) and Redruth (U2). Most journeys are worked by blue-liveried ADL Enviro400 MMCs. One loads up at Falmouth, The Moor, on an early morning journey. It was new in 2016 and is a 73-seater.*

*A batch of 20 red-liveried Tinner-branded ADL Enviro400 MMCs joined the First fleet in 2016 to operate the long interurban routes T1 (from Penzance) and T2 (from St. Ives) via Hayle, Camborne and Redruth to Truro. A single journey from end to end takes almost two hours. This bus is seen opposite Redruth railway station.*

*A First Dennis Trident with East Lancs Myllennium body climbs out of St Ives, passing the Harbour Hotel as it starts its journey to Penzance and Madron. First Devon & Cornwall purchased 13 of these buses in 2005.*

*The Mousehole service requires short and narrow vehicles. In years gone by the coastal route from Penzance via Newlyn was worked by Bristol LHSs, but nowadays Optare Solos are the choice. First operates the summer service on a 20-minute headway requiring three vehicles. A route-branded example turns on to the quayside at Mousehole as tourists take in the sea air.*

*In summer months First's Atlantic Coasters service offers the opportunity to enjoy a circular tour from Penzance, via Newlyn, Porthcurno, Lands End, Sennen Cove, St Just, Zennor, St Ives, Marazion and back to Penzance. The whole trip takes three hours and 40 minutes and many journeys are worked by open-toppers. A closed-top Volvo B7TL/Alexander ALX400 in appropriately coloured livery climbs out of the delightfully scenic spot of Sennen Cove.*

# The Unofficial **Official**
# **Photographer**

ALL PHOTOGRAPHS BY THE AUTHOR

**Mike Greenwood** relates how his camera became a useful tool when he worked for Leicester City Transport.

I am sure many of us ask ourselves how we got so interested in buses and it can be a difficult question to answer. It also intrigues other people. Just last year a Radio Leicester presenter somewhat threw me when, during a live interview he suddenly pitched in the question "Why do you love buses?" I had been taking part to promote a Leicester Transport Heritage Trust event and I can't now remember what I said at the time!

My display of affection for buses must have been apparent in my very early years because for my third Christmas, in 1957, amongst my presents from my parents was one of those very large Tri-ang double deck metal buses. My parents were never blessed with much surplus cash so they must have made

ABOVE: *This is the first photo I took as Leicester City Transport's unofficial official photographer. It is of 266, the first Metropolitan built for LCT by MCW and featuring Scania running units. Having received 35 single-deck Metro-Scanias in 1971-72 the transport department needed new double-deckers so general manager Leslie Smith ordered an initial batch of eight buses straight from the drawing board! The photo was taken on the forecourt of the Abbey Park Road depot, prior to entry into service, on April 5, 1974.*

quite a few sacrifices to be able to afford it and buy something of similar value so as not to upset my elder brother!

Apparently, I was then struck down with measles that Christmas, which badly affected me, so it was a few days later before I could open my eyes to see my new toy. I still have that bus, stored in the loft, and it has seen better days. I treated it to a somewhat crude repaint into Leicester City Transport's cream and maroon livery and transformed it, the best I could, into my favourite LCT bus – 168, a Leyland Titan PD3.

ABOVE: *In May 1974 there was discontent amongst the LCT road staff. I cannot recall whether this related to the wage rise being offered not meeting the trade union's expectations or whether it was about new duties being proposed. Whatever the reason, on May 22, 1974 there was a very rare occasion when the entire fleet was called back in to the Abbey Park Road depot at lunchtime so that the road staff could attend a meeting called by the trade union. I took this photo from the roof of the head office building and it captures a queue of 19 buses in Abbey Park Road waiting to make the right turn into the depot yard. It also shows the variety of the LCT fleet at that time with the top of an East Lancs-bodied Leyland Titan PD3A in the foreground and Metro-Scanias, Bristol REs, a Metropolitan, an AEC Renown, an Atlantean and more PD3As all waiting in the queue. The fleet returned to service following the meeting.*

LEFT: *Harry Flowers was the department's route equipment maintenance man. This role included the installation, repair, maintenance and upkeep of bus stop flags and timetable cases. Harry had joined the department in 1937 and had worked in the body shop prior to taking up his on-the-road role. As part of my traffic office duties I worked closely with him. On July 17, 1974 I found him in the depot yard at lunch time and persuaded him to pose with a new bus stop flag at the back of his van. Harry was allocated a Ford Transit with a fibreglass roof extension which allowed him to stand comfortably at a workbench installed inside. It was known as the 'ice cream van' and had the radio call sign '913'. The younger members of the traffic office thought that it should have been '99'! Harry retired in October 1977 having completed 40 years' service.*

That present may well have set the seed for my lifelong interest in buses. By the time I was considering my future career, in the early 1970s, an appointment with the school's career advisor was deemed unnecessary because for me it was only ever going to be the bus industry.

My Saturday job in the late 1960s was cleaning the coaches of local Leicester operator County Travel, and whilst I enjoyed washing the exterior of the coaches the cleaning of the interior, especially dried-up sick after some Friday night hires, was less

Leicester City Transport had undertaken quite a sizeable amount of private hire work ever since it had started operating motorbuses in 1924. However, this was mainly for transport to school playing fields and swimming baths, plus local private hires which didn't involve great distances. The bus fleet was perfectly adequate for such work. The main customer for longer distance travel was the department's recreation club which included taking the St John Ambulance team members to competitions with other municipal operators which could be as far away as Liverpool. The recreation club made a polite request to Leslie Smith asking if the purchase of a purpose-built coach might be possible which could also be used commercially. Mr Smith thought that this was a reasonable request and in October 1974 put forward a recommendation to the transport committee, but they voted against the motion by five votes to three. No doubt disappointed by this decision Leslie Smith tried again with a different approach in March 1975. This time he recommended the experimental use of a coach for the department's park-and-ride north service. His pitch to the transport committee must have been convincing because after discussion it was unanimously agreed that approval be given to purchase a suitable coach. A Duple-bodied Ford R114 was ordered and arrived in July 1975. I photographed it on July 28 in Abbey Park which was conveniently located opposite the main depot. Driver Gordon Winterburn poses with his new steed.

Leslie Smith retired at the end of September 1975 and was replaced by Geoffrey Hilditch. He was an accomplished engineer and having been annoyed by Leyland when they announced they were withdrawing the Daimler Fleetline chassis he managed to convince Hestair Dennis of the benefit of re-entering the PSV market and thus the Dennis Dominator chassis was conceived. A test bed utilising a former West Yorkshire PTE Roe-bodied Daimler CVG6 gave in-service feedback on the principal mechanical components which were to be used in the new chassis. Whilst at Leicester it was painted bright orange and became known as the Clockwork Orange. Here it waits at the service 29 Stoneygate barrier in Humberstone Gate in January 1976. The bus certainly had a notable turn of speed. The shopping centre in Humberstone Gate had a first-floor pedestrian gallery which provided a nice vantage point for bus photography.

ABOVE & INSET: *February 1979 was notable for a prolonged spell of wintry weather. On February 19 LCT's final Metro-Scania saloon, 225, which had been new in July 1972, had taken up service in the early morning in very icy conditions. Unfortunately, it was involved in a head on collision with a coach. There was quite a debate amongst the engineers as to whether they should write the bus off and it looked like that was going to be the case when a former Merthyr Tydfil Corporation Metro-Scania was acquired in March 1979. The LCT body shop, however, was then given authorisation to repair the bus and the colour photo shows the bus with the repair completed and fresh from the paint shop on May 8, 1980. This is testament to the ability and skill of the body shop personnel. If my memory serves me correctly, I believe that the driver, who was badly injured in the crash, also returned to LCT bus driving in May 1980.*

*This photo of East Lancs-bodied Leyland PD3A, fleet number 71 which was new in1965, was taken from the balcony of the accounts office which overlooked Abbey Park Road. By the time I took the photo in February 1979 I was no longer working in the accounts office but was allowed access if I asked nicely! The bus carefully negotiates the wintry conditions as it makes its way towards the City Centre from where it will continue to Eyres Monsell.*

appealing. I was pretty bright at school but further education didn't appeal so in 1970 I sent letters to Leicester City Transport and the local office of Midland Red to enquire about career prospects once I had finished my A-levels in 1972.

LCT was the first to respond and an interview was arranged with their training officer, Mr L V Pratt,

in September 1970. Career opportunities were discussed and what level of exam results I would need to be accepted by the department. Midland Red's response related to the National Bus Company management training scheme and this needed a higher level of exam results. My real interest was in Midland Red, and I wasn't too keen on the prospect

*I'm not sure why I was asked to take this photo, but it did take a bit of setting up. LCT had put me through a PSV driving test in June 1976 so it is likely I drove one of the buses across the road from the depot into the entrance area just inside Abbey Park. It was February 1980 which accounts for the long shadows. LCT had received its first Dennis Dominator in October 1977, which was the second chassis off the production line. By the time 187, in the centre of the line-up, was added to the fleet in November 1979 LCT had 35 Dominators in service. East Lancs had bodied 33 of these, with the other two receiving Marshall bodies. The Metropolitan on the left was from the final batch of five buses delivered to LCT but that had been some time earlier, in November 1977. The Metrobus on the right, however, was brand new and the first of a batch of four buses. However, the Metrobus could not challenge the Dominator's dominance and batches of the Guildford product were ordered in large quantities right up to bus deregulation in 1986.*

of the somewhat nomadic life of allocation to any one of the NBC companies. So, I decided I would pursue the Leicester City Transport option.

In the summer of 1972, I had achieved the required exam grades and contacted LCT again. The only problem was that being a relatively small organisation they didn't have any vacancies in the traffic office but were able to offer me a position in the accounts department. This came with the caveat that they would consider me as soon as a suitable position became available in the traffic office. I was pretty good at maths and I was keen to join LCT, so I accepted their offer and became an accounts clerk on 17 July 1972, working at the Abbey Park Road head office.

I soon got into the swing of things in the world of work and enjoyed my career development. Part of my duties was to visit various departments within the Abbey Park Road site, including the body, fitting and paint shops. It was like having an All Areas Pass to a favourite venue, so I was a very happy boy. I was also a keen photographer, so I was soon taking my camera to work and taking shots not generally available to other enthusiasts.

The accounts department was on the top floor of the elegant 1937 two-storey head office building. Not only that. but it was the only office to have a balcony.

This provided some unconventional photographic opportunities. As I got to know senior members of the engineering team, on occasions I was able to gain access to the flat roof of the building which allowed some semi-aerial shots of the depot yard to be taken. I was, however, careful not to abuse the privileges I was being afforded.

My enthusiasm and photographic ability were not lost on the senior members of the traffic section, but it still took almost two years before a suitable vacancy arose in their department in April 1974. This was not a particular problem for me as I was enjoying my time in the accounts office, especially the duties whereby I was arranging the re-licensing of various buses each month and checking the accuracy of MCW invoices for new Metro-Scania saloons. I also used to spend many a lunchtime,

legitimately, examining files in the engineer's administration section. I particular liked the 'Sale of Buses' folder which made fascinating reading! This went back to the 1960s and I did make some notes but how I now wished I had photocopied it all.

The general manager at Leicester City Transport when I joined was Leslie Smith. Mr Smith had joined the transport department in September 1927 as a 15-year old clerk. He had risen through the ranks taking over as the top man in 1966 following the retirement of the previous general manager, John Cooper. Leslie Smith had become highly regarded within the industry with notable achievements being the introduction of pioneering CCTV and radio control in the mid-1960s, and then in the early 1970s with vehicle evolution, initially with the revolutionary Metro-Scania saloon and then

*The next chassis which Geoffrey Hilditch assisted with the development of was the single-deck Dennis Falcon. LCT 90 had the first chassis number in the Falcon series, SDA401/101. Delivered in April 1981 it carried an attractive Duple 51-seat body. In April I photographed it with JCP 60F, which was one of the buses on loan from the Science Museum at Wroughton. This all-Leyland Lion PLSC1 spent most of its life with Jersey Motor Transport, registered J 4601. It had received the pseudo Edinburgh livery for an appearance in the 1969 film The Prime of Miss Jean Brodie. As it happens the livery fitted in quite nicely with that of LCT. The photograph was taken at the cemetery gates on Welford Road. This was a very busy road and I recall that it took a long time to wait for a clear gap in the traffic from both directions to get the photo.*

October 2, 1982 was a sad day for bus enthusiasts as LCT chose that date to end the operation of its remaining Leyland Titans. First thing that morning I had slipped into the Abbey Park Road depot and crafted an appropriate "Last LCT PD3" display on a white blank section of number 16's front destination blind. This bus had been repainted into the original livery with three maroon bands and was allocated to operate the final journey from the city centre to Nether Hall. The city's lord mayor was also to travel on the bus issuing souvenir tickets to passengers. I caught up with 16 in the central depot yard in Rutland Street just prior to it taking up duty to operate the final journey. The photo shows Geoffrey Hilditch on the left talking to operations director Bill Bishop. There were ten PD3s working on the final day, and the three shown here had already operated that final journey in service to Nether Hall, having been replaced by brand-new Dennis Dominators at the Nether Hall terminus. Mr Hilditch drove 16 for part of that last journey to Nether Hall whilst I was on board photographing the lord mayor in action. When we arrived at the Nether Hall terminus Mr Hilditch asked me if I would like to take 16 back to the Abbey Park Road depot. Whilst saddened by the PD3s demise, they had been given a great send-off, so I was happy to respond positively to the offer and what an honour it was to have that final drive!

Oops! A fitter took Metropolitan 281 out on a breakdown change-over on March 7, 1983 but unfortunately, he took the wrong route to the broken-down vehicle and collided with a low bridge in Barkby Road on the outskirts of the city. I was summoned by the engineering team to photograph the bus once it got back to Abbey Park Road depot. The bus was repaired in the body shop and re-entered service on July 26.

*In 1981 local enthusiasts encouraged me to approach Geoffrey Hilditch with the suggestion of taking back into ownership a former LCT 1950 Leyland Titan PD2. This bus had served the transport department well giving almost 20 years' service prior to its withdrawal in March 1970. The bus then served various owners in North Lincolnshire for a further 11 years but was considered by the local enthusiast fraternity to be too good to be scrapped when it reached dealer Joe Sykes in September 1981. Mr Hilditch was a little unsure at first when I approached him about the matter and asked me what I thought we would do with it if he went along with the idea. Thinking on my feet I suggested that it could be a revenue earner as part of the private hire fleet, as well as being an asset at local community events. In truth I don't think Mr Hilditch really needed much convincing and he struck a deal with Joe Sykes and the bus returned to LCT in November 1981. The engineering team did a magnificent job in restoring the bus to its former glory. This photo, which I took in the body shop in May 1983, shows it in a late stage of the restoration process. The bus made its public debut at a rally in Cardiff in June 1983 and was an immediate award winner.*

the Metropolitan double-deck, the results of the collaboration between Scania and MCW which brought car-like attributes to the bus industry with power steering, fully-automatic transmission and air suspension.

My initial role in the traffic section was to assist the traffic officer with all aspects of publicity and promotion. My arrival also coincided with LCT celebrating 50 years of motorbus operation, with part of the celebration being a souvenir publication and an open day at the Abbey Park Road depot in July 1974. Whilst LCT used commercial photographers for most of its requirements I was regularly being called on to take photos. Although this role was not listed in my job description, I had no intention of refusing these requests. Accordingly,

I became the department's 'unofficial official photographer'!

Leslie Smith retired at the end of September 1975 and was succeeded by Geoffrey Hilditch who took up his post on October 1. Mr. Hilditch had a unique approach to management, together with a deep interest in transport history and brought with him a collection of old buses to Abbey Park Road that was on loan to him from the Science Museum collection at Wroughton, near Swindon.

Mr. Hilditch was keen to utilise my photographic abilities, still in an unofficial capacity but on an ever-increasing basis, and did so until I left to join South Yorkshire PTE as part of a career move in July 1983 … but that is another story.

*Part of the 1980 Transport Act deregulated the express coach market and in May 1983 LCT teamed up with fellow municipalities Burnley & Pendle and Maidstone Borough Council to introduce a jointly-operated express coach service between Blackpool and Dover via Burnley, Halifax, Sheffield, Leicester, London and Maidstone. The route was marketed as Service 100, the City Flyer, with a daily service of four journeys in each direction. Vehicle allocation was two from Leicester and one each from Burnley and Maidstone. The photo of LCT 17, a 1982 Plaxton-bodied Leyland Tiger complete with window vinyls promoting the service, was taken at the city's De Montfort Hall concert venue in May 1983.*

# Brits Abroad
## High Capacity in Hong Kong

**Colin Douglas** illustrates a selection of the three-axle double-deckers which provide many of Hong Kong's busy bus services.

ncluding a number of outlying islands, the Hong Kong Special Administrative Region of China covers some 426 square miles, comprising Hong Kong Island, the Kowloon Peninsula and the New Territories. The combined population of the area is around 7.5 million people. Hong Kong became a British colony in 1841, to which the other areas were later added. In 1997 Hong Kong was in effect handed back to China, but under an arrangement which allows a form of devolved government to operate. English is still one of the official languages.

LEFT: *The newest type of Wright-bodied Volvos in the KMB fleet are are 90-seat tri-axle B8L models with Gemini 3 bodies. One loads on a wet evening in Nathan Road, Kowloon.*

*KMB also runs impressive ADL Enviro500 MMC models. This 80-seater was new in 2018. It is exiting Nathan Road, bound for the Star Ferry bus station. The red livery was introduced in 2017.*

*KMB subsidiary Long Win took 26 ADL Enviro500s in 2015. They are 78-seaters. One leaves the interchange at Tung Chung, Lantau Island, where there is a demand to transfer passengers from the nearby airport to the metro system which has much lower fares than the direct rail service. Note the Airbus branding.*

An ADL Enviro500 MMC in the New World First Bus fleet at North Point, Hong Kong Island. A total of 110 similar 98-seaters were delivered to the company in 2017-18.

*A pair of New World First Bus Volvo B9TLs with Wright Gemini bodies at King's Road, North Point. Twenty-five of these 90-seaters were delivered in 2016.*

Hong Kong has a strong economy based on its power as a financial and manufacturing centre. This has evolved through its low taxation and abundant supply of labour. In Kowloon there is one of the biggest container ports in the world to allow it to move its products around the globe.

There is a great disparity in income between the citizens of Hong Kong with the majority being relatively poor and a few being very high earners and even billionaires. Some 90% of daily transport trips are made on public transport, the highest percentage in the world. To meet these needs, the main form of transport is the Mass Transit Railway which has an extensive network of rail lines, underground on Hong Kong Island and on the surface in many of the mainland areas. Buses connect with the rail network at several key interchanges and stations and operate some 800 services in total. Hong Kong has its own contactless payment card, the Octopus card, for travel across all public transport systems. A novel feature is that it can be used to pay for items in shops. Many of Hong Kong's residents live in huge tower block housing which makes for good bus-operating territory.

*A 2016 Citybus Volvo B9TL with Wrightbus Gemini body makes a sharp contrast with a Hong Kong Tramways tram in Hennessey Road, Hong Kong Island.*

*Sunny Bay Interchange, Lantau Island, is the location of this view of a Citybus ADL Enviro500 MMC. New in 2019 it is a 92-seater. Citybus has purchased almost 700 Enviro500s since 2013.*

On the north of Hong Kong Island there is also a small tram network, dating from 1904, on which some 160 quirky double-deck trams operate. There also is extensive use made of public light buses (minibuses) and taxis. A passenger ferry service, the Star Ferry, connects Hong Kong Island to Kowloon and there are now tunnels under the harbour for vehicles. Modern bridges connect the main islands in Kowloon and the New Territories. Ferry services connect the smaller islands and there is now a bridge and tunnel link to Macau, across the Pearl River estuary. This all adds to interest for the transport enthusiast. Private car use is not entirely discouraged so the net effect is a congested road network.

The main bus services in Hong Kong are operated on a government-controlled franchise, with all services having a specified route, fares, operating hours and schedule. The buses themselves are owned and operated by the respective companies and these currently number five. Services in specific areas are grouped together into individual franchises. Franchises

last for ten years and tendering is carried out for subsequent ten-year contracts.

Bus operations have evolved in Hong Kong over the years, with Kowloon Motor Bus (KMB) having the franchise for the mainland areas and China Motor Bus (CMB) for the island from soon after the Second World War. CMB gradually lost many of its services, these passing to other operators which had started up, mainly because of local dissatisfaction with CMB. Its franchise was eventually terminated in 1998, with many of its services passing to a new company, New World First Bus. FirstGroup briefly owned 26% of the company, until 2000. The other operators which had started up were New Lantao Bus Company, serving the New Territories; Citybus, serving the island, and Long Win Bus serving the new international airport which opened in 1998. The airport was built on reclaimed land on the island of Chep Lap Kok with all necessary new rail and roads infrastructure. Stagecoach briefly owned Citybus from 1999 until 2003 and Long Win Bus is owned by KMB. Further recent ownership changes have seen Citybus, New World First and New Lantao Bus come under the same ownership. There are a few additional smaller companies now too, including the MTR Corporation which provides feeder services to the rail network in the New Territories.

Buses of British heritage have long featured in Hong Kong, too many to mention. These have ranged from front-engined single-and double-deck buses bought after the Second World War through to the second-hand Daimler Fleetlines bought from London Transport, to the modern air-conditioned three-axle double-deck buses of today. Small numbers of two-axle double-deck and single-deck buses are also operated. Non-British buses feature in smaller numbers.

Air-conditioned buses were introduced gradually from 1995 and low-floor buses as they became available. All of the major fleets now meet these criteria, with the exception of part of the New Lantao Bus fleet which must use high-floor coaches due to the difficult hilly roads it operates over in the centre of Lantau Island. Recently NLB has added some brand-new double-deck buses to its fleet to serve the expanding residential areas on the flatter part of Lantau Island. Hong Kong has been slow to try hybrid or electric buses although a few from mainland China manufacturer BYD were trialled recently. More are set to follow.

Recently the major fleets have tended to buy ADL Tridents, ADL Enviros and Volvos with Alexander Dennis or Wrightbus bodies for their double-deck bus needs and YoungMan, Volvo or ADL Enviro single-deck buses. They regularly buy small quantities of other types, for example Scanias, for comparison purposes. Some MANs are also appearing in the smaller fleets.

At the time of my visit to the region last year, the combined fleets of the five main franchised operators represented around 6,000 vehicles on the road covering more than 600 routes, KMB has by far the lion's share but the variety of liveries and operators adds an impressive angle to an already colourful vista.

*Not all of Hong Kong's double-deckers are British. New Lantao Bus's recent purchases have been MAN Lion's City ND363Fs with 86-seat bodies by Malaysian builder Gemilang. One of 29 delivered in 2018 leaves the interchange at Tung Chung.*

# In the Vanguard

The autumn of 1979 saw Wadham Stringer enter the real bus market with the Vanguard, its neat appearance contrasting with previous utilitarian designs. **David Jukes** examines the Vanguard and its successors.

It was a lead article in *Buses* in August 1980 announcing the Volvo Vanguard – the combination of Wadham Stringer's then newly-introduced Vanguard bodywork and Volvo's B58 chassis – that made your then 12-year-old writer realise there was a bus bodybuilder not overly distant from his Portsmouth home.

This knowledge was cemented by the City of Portsmouth's 1982 purchase of three Vanguard-bodied Dennis Lancet midibuses. These, its last new motorbuses, offered an interesting comparison with its first – ten 1919 Thornycroft J-type open-top double-deckers bodied by Wadham Brothers. The last amalgamated with Wiltshire-based Stringer Motors in 1968 to create Wadham Stringer, but we must first go back to 1905.

## Wadham Brothers

Harold Wadham's cycle business in Stakes Hill Road, Waterlooville, expanded into a newly built workshop in 1905. Younger brother Wilfred soon

joined him to form the Wadham Brothers' Motor Company.

The building of commercial vehicle bodies was followed by interest in the growing passenger vehicle industry, the company gaining the Portsmouth Corporation order in 1919. This led to a single-deck range and an agreement to build bodies for Thornycroft which lasted until 1931. The company also built an ambulance for the St John Ambulance service in the mid-1920s; such vehicles became a major business, particularly during the post war years.

New coach and bus designs followed in the 1930s before their production ceased during World War Two. It duly resumed but Wadham Brothers' output was focused on ambulances and specialist commercial vehicles.

The 1955 launch of a PSV-converted Morris J2 van was followed by a 1957 reformation as Wadham Bros (Coachbuilders) Ltd and a new range of van conversions. Their popularity with the London local

LEFT: *Three Vanguard-bodied Dennis Lancet midibuses were delivered to the City of Portsmouth in 1982. This one is seen later in life with the council-owned Portsmouth City Transport business.* DAVID JUKES

RIGHT: *The Borough of Darlington acquired six dual-door Vanguard-bodied Ward Dalesman GRXIs in 1983-84. This one is seen in the town centre in 1988.* DAVID JUKES

authorities led to the construction of purpose-built welfare bodies.

A need for more space saw a new factory opened in Hambledon Road during 1962; the former Wadham Brothers premises were demolished four years later and replaced by a shopping precinct.

## Wadham Stringer

Wadham Stringer (Coachbuilders) Ltd was formed on the 1968 amalgamation of Wadham Brothers with Stringer Motors. It expanded with the 1972 purchase of J H Sparshatt & Sons' Portsmouth operations, which built similar products. This initially separate entity – Wadham Stringer Sparshatt (Portsmouth) Ltd then Wadham Stringer Commercials (Coachbuilders) Ltd – arguably produced its best-known products in 1975 on converting three British Airways Leyland Nationals to half-cab airside coaches.

Wadham Stringer was acquired by Tozer, Kemsley and Milbourn (Holdings) Ltd in late-1979 and formed a separate entity in the TKM automotive division.

## Vanguard

The Wadham Stringer Vanguard debuted at the 1979 Scottish Motor Show on a prototype Leyland Cub chassis. It was built using a welded square-section tubular steel structure, its modular construction intended to maximise available lengths and passenger door locations.

Standard features included a roof-mounted ventilation system; air was taken in through a rear pod, distributed by passenger-controlled overhead ventilators then expelled from a smaller forward-mounted pod. This could be supplemented by sliding window ventilators. The external trim featured plastics, particularly for the distinctive

*Awaiting departure from Guildford's Friary Bus Station is one of Tillingbourne's pair of 1983 Vanguard-bodied Dennis Dorchesters.* ROGER WATTS

ABOVE: *This Vanguard II-bodied Leyland Swift started life as a bus with Luton & District in 1989. It was upgraded with coach seats by Tantivy Blue Coach Tours for operation on Jersey.* DAVID JUKES

RIGHT: *In 2008, Autocar of Five Oak Green operated this1994 Winchester-bodied Dennis Dart which was one of three supplied to the London Borough of Redbridge.* DAVID JUKES

ends, grille, headlamp surrounds and bumpers. A deep windscreen and side windows were fitted beneath a shallow arched roof.

The prototype 8m-long Cub was followed by a 9m Ford R1014 conversion used as a Ford demonstrator. The next Vanguards were almost unrecognisable as such – six 12m semi-trailers for Dubai Airport.

Volvo combined with Wadham Stringer to produce the Volvo Vanguard, using the bus version of Volvo's B58 chassis. This acted as a Volvo demonstrator before being sold to Ayrshire Bus Owners (A1 Service) member Hunter in April 1981.

The first Vanguards to be supplied to a bus operator were built in 1981 – five 11m Bedford YMTs for Maidstone Borough Council which featured 61 passenger seats thanks to eight rows of three-plus-two seating. Other early orders gave an indication of the Vanguard's versatility with ten short Bedford YMQ-Ss for Eastern National, a 10m Dennis Lancet for Tillingbourne and a solitary Bristol LHS for Harvey of Mousehole.

The variety of chassis increased during the Vanguard's production run. Three forward-entrance Bedford SB5 coaches were dispatched to Jersey in 1985 (two for Holiday Tours and one for Pioneer Coaches). More Bedford YMTs were bodied for Maidstone in 1982 and for Metrobus of Orpington in 1986.

The heavy-duty Dennis Dorchester was more commonly used for coaches but two were bodied as service buses for Tillingbourne in 1983. The same year saw the rear-engined Dennis Falcon bodied for three operators – Grimsby-Cleethorpes acquired four Falcon H models with single-door bodies, Hartlepool six dual-door Falcon HCs (the first dual-door Vanguards built) and Alder Valley a single dual-purpose HC. The last of these was rebodied with an identical Vanguard body in 1987 after its first was destroyed by fire.

Further Dennis Lancets were bodied for Tillingbourne, Brewer of Caerau, and Hestair-Dennis – the last for demonstration duties. Two municipalities ordered the shortest 8.2m Lancet – Portsmouth (three) and Merthyr Tydfil (two).

The 1980 Ford demonstrator was followed by a second, also on an R1014 chassis. The upgraded Ford R1015 was later bodied for Jersey Motor Transport with 14 supplied between 1984 and 1987. Of similar specification was a single dual-purpose R1015 for Ralph's of Longford's Heathrow transfer work.

Just two Leyland Tigers were given Vanguard bodies for stage-carriage use, A1 Service member McKinnon acquiring these in 1982. Other less usual applications were nine Scania BR112DH buses for Newport Transport; their vertically mounted transverse rear engines required additional body bracing, centrally positioned emergency exits and stepped waistlines – the last also featured on the Hartlepool and Alder Valley Falcons.

A single front-engined Volvo B57 was bodied for Ralph's for evaluation against its Ford-based fleet at Heathrow, while alphabetically last in the chassis listings are the six dual-doored Ward Dalesman GRXIs acquired by the Borough of Darlington in 1983-84. Their Seddon Pennine RU-inspired chassis featured a straight ramped frame which created steep exit steps.

The Vanguard saw great use within the military and welfare markets. The Ministry of Defence acquired examples on AEC Reliance, Bedford VAS, Dodge G13, Leyland Leopard and Leyland Tiger chassis. Local authorities utilised far more chassis types: Bedford SB, VAS, YMQ and YMT; Dodge G08, G10 and G13; Ford R1014, R1015, R1114 and R1115; and the Leyland Cub – the last favoured in and around London. British Airways acquired Dodge G10s for aircrew transport and the Atomic Weapons Establishment had two dual-doored Bedford YMTs as Aldermaston staff buses.

### Vanguard II

The run up to bus deregulation saw Wadham Stringer announce an updated Vanguard in spring 1986. The Vanguard II featured flat sides, square cornered windows, and a new front with deeper two-piece windscreen. Options included high-backed seats and luggage racks as it was considered suitable for short-distance coaching.

The prototype was built on an extended Renault Dodge G10 chassis to allow a front entrance, albeit with significant engine intrusion. But the Vanguard II is arguably best linked to the Leyland Swift, a compact underfloor-engined chassis derived from the Roadrunner truck. The very first Swift was Vanguard II bodied as a Leyland demonstrator,

*People's Provincial H523 CTR was one of two ACE Cougars built and the only example to receive a Portsdown body. It is seen in Portsmouth city centre in August 1991. As well as ACE and Cougar badges, it carries lettering above the nearside headlamp which reads 'Portsdown by Wadham Stringer'.* DAVID JUKES

while the third went to Pioneer Coaches of St Helier in April 1987, since when several of the combination, both new and second-hand, have seen service on Jersey. The Vanguard II-bodied Swift was also snapped up by a variety of UK bus operators including Harrogate Independent, Luton & District and Stevenson's of Uttoxeter.

The Vanguard II shared its predecessor's versatility with examples built on a single Bedford SB for Pioneer Coaches and – at the opposite extreme – two Dennis Dorchesters for Amos of Daventry. Eastbourne Borough Council acquired two Dennis Javelins in 1991-92 and three Dennis Lances in 1992-93 – the last unusually fitted with high floors.

Coach & Bus '93 saw a Vanguard II-bodied Iveco TurboCity U on display, one of six built for Iveco-Ford Truck. The hoped-for market failed to materialise; Jones of Pontypridd, Wilson of Ratby, Lucketts of Watford, De Courcey of Coventry and Elsey of Gosberton took those six between them. The following year's Brighton Coach Rally saw the Iveco Countrybus launched as a Vanguard II-bodied coach for Blue Coach Tours of St Helier.

The military and welfare sectors again dominated production. The MoD acquired large numbers of 8.5, 10 and 12m Dennis Javelins, while welfare operators took examples on Bedford YMT, Dennis Javelin, Dennis Lancet, Iveco 79.14, Leyland Swift, and Renault PP160 and PP180. Many of the Renaults had centre entrances.

## Wessex

Closely following the Vanguard II in 1986 was a new minibus body, the Wessex, intended for the Freight Rover/Leyland DAF Sherpa, Renault S56, Iveco Dailybus and a variety of Mercedes chassis. A similar but lighter gauge ring frame was used. Distinguishing features were large rounded side windows and arrow-shaped quarter-lights. However, the Wessex formed a relatively minor part of the minibus market, and most PSV applications were built on Mercedes T2 chassis-cowls. Wadham Stringer used a Mercedes 709D as a demonstrator, with Plymouth Citybus acquiring two in 1990 and Ede of Par a solitary example the following year. The larger Mercedes 811D was chosen by Yellow Buses of Bournemouth for 20 31-seat minibuses in 1989. These ran for a very short period before being sold to Buffalo Travel of Flitwick and Brighton & Hove following public criticism.

A Renault S56 was used by Wadham Stringer for demonstration duties while People's Provincial acquired six on Iveco 59.12 chassis in 1993. Wessex-bodied Freight Rover, Mercedes and Renault chassis were also sold in the welfare sector.

*Running alongside the River Torridge in Bideford in August 2017 is a Taw and Torridge 10m-long Vanguard III-bodied Dennis Javelin which had been new to the Ministry of Defence.* DAVID JUKES

ABOVE: *In 1996 Southern Vectis took six 8.5m-long UVG Urbanstar-bodied Dennis Darts. This bus, seen when new, shows the distinctive direction indicators on the corners of the front dome, and the curved lower edge to the nearside windscreen.* SJB

RIGHT: *Chalkwell of Sittingbourne acquired two S320-bodied Dennis Javelins in late 1997, the first of which is seen crossing Westminster Bridge in September 2005.* DAVID JUKES

## Winchester

The Winchester coach body was introduced at the 1989 Southampton Coach Rally. It shared the Vanguard II's structure but with a large single-piece windscreen, fixed tinted side windows and new front grille. At 2.4m the body was wider than its contemporaries, enabling fitting out with full soft trim for middle-distance work.

It was initially solely available on the Leyland Swift chassis, although examples of the nine-metre Dennis Dart were later bodied. The Winchester was far from common despite Wadham Stringer's best hopes. Those on Swift chassis were built for Wadham Stringer as a demonstrator and the London Boroughs of Lewisham (two including an ex-demonstrator) and Waltham Forest (three). The Darts were a demonstrator, one for the United States Army, plus three for the London Borough of Redbridge and two for Rotherham Metropolitan Borough Council.

There was also a one-off MAN 11.190-based Winchester displayed at ExpoCoach in 1994 before later delivery to Coles of Eversley. Its higher waistline required shallower side windows than standard.

## Portsdown

The sale in 1989 of the Duple Dartline body to Carlyle saw Dennis make its Dart chassis available to other bodybuilders. Wadham Stringer offered the first alternative with the steel framed Portsdown, named after a local Portsmouth landmark. Its conventional styling was designed to ease maintenance with gasket-mounted square-cornered windows and a two-piece double curvature windscreen. The Portsdown was also available on the ACE Cougar, also a rear-engined city bus but with a ramped rather than stepped saloon floor.

The prototype Portsdown was built in 1990 on an 8.5m Dart chassis and used as a demonstrator before sale to Southampton Citybus. Other 1990 sales were three nine-metre Darts to Eastbourne

*By coincidence matching route and registration numbers are carried by National Express West Midlands 1520 (R120 XOB). This was one of nine Mercedes-Benz O405Ns fitted out by UVG for Travel West Midlands in 1998. It is seen in Birmingham city centre in 2010.* DAVID JUKES

Borough (two) and Jim Stone of Glazebury (one), plus the sole ACE Cougar to be bodied by Wadham Stringer which was for People's Provincial.

Just 12 more Portsdown bodies were built – four nine-metre Darts, three demonstrators and one for East Surrey of Godstone, and eight 9.8m Darts, two for Eastbourne Borough, one for the St Christopher's Coach Fund, two for Fuggles of Benenden and three for Wealden of Five Oak Green.

## Wessex II

Parent company TKM was acquired by Inchcape PLC in 1992. Its new owners sold Wadham Stringer (Coachbuilders) Ltd to the Universal Vehicles Group (UVG) on August 13, 1993. UVG renamed its acquisition WS Coachbuilders Ltd because Wadham Stringer remained active under Inchcape ownership.

The improved Wessex II was introduced soon after the ownership change. A Cromweld stainless steel frame was used for the widened bodywork which now featured shorter square-cornered side windows. Least usual were 20 dual-door Iveco 59.12 minibuses for Devon General, delivered in summer 1994. More numerous were the Mercedes 709D and 811D, with a concentration in western and central

Scotland – Davidson of Whitburn, HAD of Shotts, Marbill of Beith, McDade of Uddingston and Ashton of Port Glasgow buying in quantity. English buyers included Pathfinder of Newark, Stevenson's of Uttoxeter and Tillingbourne of Cranleigh.

## Vanguard III / Unistar

Almost creeping under the radar in 1994 was the Vanguard III, developed for MoD contracts. It was built on the Dennis Javelin to full PSV specification which offered a degree of anonymity for security purposes and better resale values. The Vanguard III included a new front end featuring a plain dash, two-piece double curvature windscreen and raked roof dome.

UVG renamed WS Coachbuilders as the UVG Bus Division and moved ambulance production to Brighouse in autumn 1995. The Vanguard III was simultaneously renamed Unistar and marketed more widely with a restyled front. It was initially available on the 12-metre Dennis Javelin with the first pair acquired by Mayne of Manchester; other buyers included Whittle of Kidderminster and Metcalfe of Sedgefield. Coles of Eversley bought a single 8.5m Javelin. Most Unistars were built for the MoD.

## Citystar

The other WS product retained under the UVG brand was the Wessex II minibus, which was renamed the Citystar. It remained available on Iveco 59.12 and Mercedes chassis. Examples of the former were acquired by Anslow of Pontypool and Blue Bus of Middleton, among others. Mercedes were more numerous with ten 711Ds for Rhondda Buses in late-1995 followed by Ashton of Port Glasgow with two 709Ds, three 711Ds and one 811D in 1996. Other buyers included Red Rose of Aylesbury, Tillingbourne of Cranleigh, Wealden of Five Oak Green and Epsom Coaches.

Citystar production moved to UVG's Bedwas plant in late-1997.

## Urbanstar

The Portsdown was unsuccessful, and UVG introduced the John Worker-designed Urbanstar as its replacement. This used a Cromweld stainless steel frame with curvature a distinct styling theme.

The Urbanstar featured curved edges to the leading and trailing deeper side windows and a drooped nearside windscreen. Roof-mounted beacons encasing side-facing indicators were fitted fore and aft.

The first Urbanstars were built on 9.8m Dennis Darts for People's Provincial with six delivered after the company's sale to FirstBus. Identical buses were received by Gascoigne of Sandford, Red Rose of Aylesbury, Flightparks of Horley and the Isle of Wight County Council. Southern Vectis bought the only 8.5m Urbanstar-bodied Darts, its six arriving in April 1996.

UVG built two prototype low-floor Urbanstars on Dennis Dart SLF chassis in September and December 1996 before production deliveries commenced from January 1997. The jig-assembled body's exterior remained essentially unchanged – the windscreen was mounted lower – causing the forward waistline to align above the seatbacks rather than below thanks to a lower floor – shorter passengers now had to peer out!

Bulk buyers of the new Urbanstar included Aviation Defence at Heathrow (eight), Mackie of Alloa (four), Kelvin Central bought 14 of them as did Solent Blue Line franchisee Marchwood Motorways; Jones of Pontypridd bought eight and Williams of Crossways had seven. Concluding sales took place in 1998 and 1999 – the most unusual being a Northamptonshire Fire Service command unit.

## S320

The Unistar was reworked in 1997 as the S320. The front end featured a large curved windscreen, high intensity headlights and new entrance door. Rectangular pipes located aft of the cab/entrance served as visual separators from the passenger area while channelling rainwater. Bonded double-glazed side windows were fitted.

The coach was intended for local duties and was initially offered on 12m Dennis Javelins; optional other lengths were not taken up during its short production run. Just 41 were built during UVG's ownership. Aviation Defence acquired six, Chalkwell of Sittingbourne two and Whittle of Kidderminster six (one a rebody), with other operators buying single examples. Some determined the Javelin/S320 combination as being ideal for school duties and specified three-plus-two seating, increasing capacity to 69 or 72 – Corbel of

ABOVE: *The UVG Urbanstar became the Caetano Compass, as seen on this Dennis Dart operating for Arriva the Shires in Reading in 2012. It had been new to Limebourne of London as T406 LGP in 1999. It reached Arriva via MK Metro.* DAVID JUKES

BELOW: *On route to Horsham town centre from the town's railway station in March 2012 is a Metrobus Caetano Nimbus-bodied Dennis Dart SLF. The bus was new in 2001.* DAVID JUKES

*Connex took delivery of 13 Nimbus Slimbus-bodied Alexander Dennis Dart SLFs in April 2007. They were 10m-long 41-seaters.*
DAVID JUKES

Edgware acquired four, with Horseman of Reading and West of Woodford Green buying one each.

Local authorities also bought the S320 – Isle of Wight County Council, the London Boroughs of Brent and Havering, and Rotherham Metropolitan Borough Council.

### Mercedes-Benz O405N

The late 1990s found Mercedes keen to supply the British bus market with large buses. Its O405N was chosen, available as an underframe or complete vehicle. Its more basic continental specification led Mercedes to supply the UK with running shells for fitting out by chosen partner UVG. A prototype was followed by the first nine for Travel West Midlands, but all was not well at Waterlooville.

UVG's bus division called in the receivers during December 1997 soon after a reshuffle which switched Citystar production to South Wales. The remaining O405Ns were instead finished by Mercedes at its Barnsley premises while UVG sought a buyer.

### Compass

UVG's bus division was acquired by Salvador Caetano (UK) for £2million in early 1998. Production was maintained at Waterlooville under the new ownership and the Urbanstar continued as the Caetano Compass, essentially the same product on Dennis Dart SLF chassis.

Early sales to Newcastle Airport and Williams of Crosskeys were followed by no fewer than 34 for Limebourne of Battersea to operate London tendered routes, and Jones of Pontypridd (seven) among smaller orders for other operators. The last to enter service were nine for the Status Group in 2001.

### Cutlass

S320 production also continued at Waterlooville after it was re-engineered as the Caetano Compass – the distinctive vertical rectangular pipes were no more. Production remained standardised on the 12-metre Javelin built by Dennis, TransBus and Alexander Dennis during the Cutlass's 1999-2004 production. Most of the 46 built were high-capacity coaches with three-plus-two seating; principal buyers were Norfolk County Council with 22 between 1999 and 2003, plus Lincolnshire County Council and Thomas of Porth – each with four.

## Nimbus

The Caetano Nimbus was an aluminium-framed body which ultimately replaced the Compass. It was built solely on the Dennis/TransBus/Alexander Dennis Dart SLF chassis and featured a deep cantrail and upright profile. Hints of the Portuguese parent's styling were evident in the curved dash panel and angled headlights.

The Nimbus debuted at 1999's Coach & Bus show in the form of a demonstrator. The first production

ABOVE: *Shirley Road, Southampton, on a sunny day in September 2012 sees a Blue Star 2001 Nimbus-bodied Dart SLF, heading towards the city centre and Thornhill. It was new to Minerva Accord, passing to Blue Star when it won the Uni-link contract in 2008.* DAVID JUKES

BELOW: *Exhibited at the 2006 Showbus rally was the first of two pre-production Caetano-bodied Scania K310UD tri-axle low-floor double-deckers built at Waterlooville for Kowloon Motor Bus of Hong Kong. Twenty production vehicles followed the initial pair, but they were built in Portugal as Salvador Caetano had ceased UK manufacture.* DAVID JUKES

vehicles went to Cheney of Banbury the following year with other early recipients including White Rose of Staines, Amos of Daventry, Claribel of Birmingham, and Williams of Crosskeys.

Several London operators also chose the Nimbus for tendered routes; Hackney Community Transport (11), Sullivan of Potters Bar (seven), Blue Triangle of Rainham (eight), Tellings Golden Miller took 45 plus six for its Linkline subsidiary, Docklands Minibuses (12), First Capital (34), CentreWest (19) and Ealing Community Transport (13).

Other buyers included Silcox of Pembroke Dock (three), First Midland Red (five), Minerva Accord (ten for Southampton Unilink services), and De Courcey of Coventry (four).

## Nimbus Slimbus

A 2.3m-wide version of the Nimbus, known as the Nimbus Slimbus, was developed for Jersey in 2002. Thirty-three Dart SLF 29-seaters were delivered to Connex that autumn, followed by 19 longer 41-seaters between 2004 and 2007.

The Slimbus saw service elsewhere with Hackney Community Transport acquiring nine for London tendered routes, and the Gibraltar Bus Company taking 18, the only left-hand-drive examples built. Token numbers were acquired by Bu-Val of Smithybridge, Renown of Bexhill, Irvine of Law and SM Coaches of Harlow. The type also proved popular for airport car park duties where its narrow width proved invaluable.

## The Final Fling

Two prototype Caetano-bodied Scania K310UD double-deckers were constructed at Waterlooville for Kowloon Motor Bus of Hong Kong. They entered service in March 2007 and February 2008 – the first after the 2006 Showbus exhibition. These were the only double-deckers built at the Hambledon Road factory as an overly competitive market forced Salvador Caetano to cease production at Waterlooville in 2007, the factory was instead retained as Caetano's repair and servicing centre until final closure.

Planning permission for a retail park on the factory site was granted by Havant Borough Council in July 2011 with its demolition occurring in spring 2012.

With grateful thanks for their kind assistance to John Horn (who was bus and coach sales manager at Wadham Stringer from 1990-93 and UVG 1995-96) and Roger Watts.

# Preparing for the
# Future

Are the days of diesel power coming to an end? **Richard Walter** illustrates buses powered by a selection of alternative technologies.

The appearance and performance of the traditional bus worldwide has been changing quite dramatically over the last few years. Operators have worked hard to reduce emissions and meet government climate change targets. Euro 6 compliant buses emit considerably lower levels of harmful exhaust gases than their predecessors.

To achieve even lower emissions there have been trials of hybrid, hydrogen, electric and gas vehicles up and down the country. The availability of so many cleaner choices has resulted in sizeable purchases for fleets with some operators moving towards total replacement of diesel buses.

In this article I look at some of the many developments in recent years. Yet even as I write, 2020 has witnessed the unthinkable consequences of coronavirus spreading across the world and the bus and coach industry has taken a substantial economical knock. How this will reflect on future orders and indeed on how the established companies and manufacturers will recover is uncertain. There could be many unforeseen changes ahead.

ABOVE: *Chinese manufacturer Yutong offers electric buses in the UK through its distributor, Pelican Bus and Coach. Orders for 2020 delivery have been placed by Go North East, which is taking nine, and McGill's of Greenock, with one. This E10 demonstrator in London livery was displayed at Coach & Bus in November 2019.*

*Tower Transit operates two Van Hool A330 hydrogen fuel cell buses. BH63102 (LJ67 HTG) crosses London's Waterloo Bridge on route RV1 to Tower Gateway, a service which has since been withdrawn.*

ABOVE: *Lothian Buses purchased six Wright StreetAir electric buses in 2017. Here 286 (SK67 FLE) is seen at Eastfield terminus providing a part route 26 on a vintage bus running day prior to formally entering service. All but two of the buses had been withdrawn by the end of 2019.*

BELOW: *Belarusian manufacturer Belkommunmash launched its prototype right-hand drive E4200P electric bus at the 2019 Coach & Bus show at the National Exhibition Centre. The bus is fitted with fast-charging supercapacitors and is set to go on trial with Nottingham operator CT4N during 2020.*

ABOVE: *Pictured in the centre of Dundee is Xplore Dundee's ADL Enviro400 MMC SmartHybrid 6679 (SN69 ZNR). It features route branding for services five, nine and ten. Xplore Dundee is part of National Express which this year announced that it intends to buy no more diesel buses and aims to have a zero-emission bus fleet by 2030.*

ABOVE CENTRE: *First Glasgow acquired two BYD ADL Enviro200EV electric buses in January 2020 for use on route M3 between the city centre and the northern suburb of Milton. The livery reflects the partnership with, and funding from, SP Energy Networks. Glasgow aims to be the UK's first net zero carbon city by 2030.*

BELOW: *Towards the end of 2019 London claimed to have the largest fleet of electric buses in Europe, with over 200 in service. Various London operators have been investing in ADL BYD Enviro200 MMC electric buses. Go Ahead London SEe86 (LA19 KBN) was photographed on route 214 near Camden Town.*

ABOVE RIGHT: *To reduce the city's carbon footprint, Aberdeen took part in fuel cell trials with ten buses split between Stagecoach Bluebird and First Aberdeen. Included in the trial was the UK's first hydrogen production and bus refuelling station at Kittybrewster. This Van Hool A330 hydrogen fuel cell vehicle 29901 (SV14 DMX) was one of the Stagecoach examples. The buses were withdrawn in January 2020 marking the end of the first phase of the programme. What are thought to be the world's first hydrogen fuel cell double-deckers – 15 Wrightbus vehicles – were planned to enter service with First Aberdeen in 2020.*

BELOW: *In 2018, the mayor of London, Sadiq Khan, announced the creation of the largest double-deck electric fleet in Europe. Metroline received 31 Optare Metrodecker EVs specifically for route 134 between Warren Street and Finchley. Here OME2652 (YJ19 HVC) is passing through Camden Town shortly after delivery in the summer of 2019. Tower Transit ordered 37 similar buses this year.*

*First York 49905 (YJ14 BHK) is an Optare Versa V1100EV seen on park-and-ride duties in the city. A new blue livery is being introduced and articulated buses used on the service are to be replaced during 2020 by Optare Metrodecker EVs.*

*Some companies now favour larger capacity double and single-deckers which retain diesel engines but can carry more passengers per litre of fuel consumed. ADL Enviro400XLB-bodied Volvo B8L 1069 (SJ19 OWC), is one of 78 triaxles operated by Lothian Buses, most of which have 100 seats. It was photographed with Edinburgh's Arthur's Seat in the background. Stagecoach purchased similar vehicles in 2020.*

LEFT: *Five BYD Auto K8SR electric buses were delivered to Metroline in 2016 and evaluated in service until 2019. These included BYD1472 (LJ16 EZN) in Oxford Circus in the summer of 2018. The livery with green leaves has been used on several hybrids and other low-emission buses in London.*

BELOW: *Interest in the use of gas to fuel buses has waxed and waned over the years. Currently Scania is the main proponent of gas and this demonstration biogas fuelled N280UD with ADL Enviro400 MMC body has the apt registration DD16 GAS. It is seen running for Reading Buses, which operates over 60 gas-powered Scania single- and double-deckers.*
GAVIN BOOTH

# A tale of two cities: Glasgow

## You'll have had your buses

**Gavin Booth,** Edinburgh born and bred, looks at Glasgow.

There's a joke that when an unexpected visitor arrives at a door in Glasgow the welcome is 'Come in and have some tea.' In Edinburgh it's 'Come in, you'll have had your tea.' I think it's a joke. But then I was born and bred in Edinburgh.

There has long been a jokey rivalry between Edinburgh and Glasgow. We Edinburghers are supposed to be quiet and reserved while Glaswegians are friendly and outgoing – the Scots word is gallus – bold, cheeky, flashy. My good friend Stewart J Brown, editor of this splendid publication, is an unashamed Glaswegian and for more than half a century we have traded friendly jokes so for this Yearbook we agreed to write about each other's cities, from an unbiased point of view, obviously. Possibly. So here goes.

Glasgow is just 45 miles east of Edinburgh – not far enough, some might say – and today is a 45-minute train journey. In the 1950s, when the trains took a

*Springtime in George Square in 1967 and one of 175 similar Leyland Titans with Alexander bodies delivered to Glasgow Corporation in 1958-60 en route to Scotstoun West; the Corporation built a further 75 similar bodies on Titan chassis at its Coplawhill Works. It is passing a Scottish Omnibuses Bristol Lodekka.*

ALL PHOTOGRAPHS BY THE AUTHOR OR
FROM THE AUTHOR'S COLLECTION

ABOVE: *Well-filled 1939-built Glasgow Coronation car 1246 in what I believe to be Argyle Street in 1960, while a single prospective passenger obeys the instruction and queues on the other side of the sign.*

RIGHT: *For an Edinburgher, one of the main attractions at Glasgow's highly successful Garden Festival in 1988 was the opportunity to ride on preserved Edinburgh Corporation domed-roof standard tram 35, new in 1948. There were also apparently three Glasgow cars and a Blackpool car ...*

great deal longer, my parents took my wee sister and myself through to Glasgow for the first time, probably on an Edinburgh Monday holiday. I was into trains in a big way so that was a treat, as was our first sight of, and ride on, an escalator – a wooden one, admittedly, but almost certainly the first in Scotland. This was in Lewis's Argyle Street department store.

But I was more entranced by the trams outside in Argyle Street. After our stately madder and white trams in Edinburgh, these green, yellow, and cream beasts were a revelation. And in Glasgow in the early 1950s the trams just kept coming, elderly-looking standard cars that really were as old as they looked, and flashy streamlined monsters – Coronations and Cunarders, big bogie cars that looked huge and impressive. And of course, they were big: 34ft 6in long compared with Edinburgh's 30ft four-wheel standard cars.

## The Travelling Teen

In my teens I was allowed to travel through to Glasgow on my own, memorably visiting the 1957 Scottish Motor Show at Kelvin Hall and, prompted by articles in *Buses Illustrated*, which by then was essential reading, I ventured into Glasgow's east end to find the Lowland Motorways depot at Shettleston, home of the two Leyland LFDD prototypes that paved the way for the Atlantean. Neither was in service the day I visited, but that was fine because I was able to inspect them at the depot. More formal visits to depots in and around Glasgow followed when I joined the newly created Scottish branch of The Omnibus Society, making a whole host of new friends with similar interest, including the previously mentioned Mr Brown.

I have a constantly nagging regret that Edinburgh withdrew most of its first-generation trams before I was even a teenager and while I travelled on

*Following the closure of Glasgow's once-great tramway the corporation started to invest in substantial deliveries of Alexander-bodied Leyland Atlanteans. LA43, new in 1962, is in George Square, dominated by the Sir Walter Scott monument, more conventional than Edinburgh's Gothic equivalent. Note the Leyland-Albion badge on the front of the Atlantean, a nod to the Albion buses built in Glasgow.*

them for years, I took precious few photographs of them – four, in fact, on father's Box Brownie. So, I resolved to sample and photograph as many of Glasgow's remaining trams in the years up to their final withdrawal in 1962. Day trips and enthusiast tours allowed me to do this, and I enjoyed many exhilarating rides to parts of Glasgow that were, shall we say, off the tourist trail. And just as I had travelled on Edinburgh's last tram procession in 1956, I managed to get a place on the Glasgow procession six years later.

Glasgow still had trolleybuses and I enjoyed chasing these on my own account and on organised tours. But now I was mainly concentrating on the motorbuses. Glasgow had received one of the first production Leyland Atlanteans and so it was essential to find it and ride on it; this, remember, was in the days when you had to have the patience to search out interesting buses without the advantage of a mobile phone telling you where every bus is at any given time. And what place-names – Glasgow seemed to go in for long three-and-four-syllable place-names: Bellahouston, Carmunnock, Carnwadric,

*Glasgow only operated trolleybuses from 1949 to 1967, and the last deliveries, in 1957-58, were 90 of these stylish Crossley-bodied BUT 9613T.*

Keppochhill, Pollokshields (not to be confused with Pollokshaws), Thornliebank – and everybody's favourite, Auchenshuggle.

One of the joys of Glasgow was – and to a degree still is –the sheer variety of operators, vehicle types and liveries. The green/cream/orange Glasgow Corporation trams were easily found in the city

*Some Western SMT routes used Clyde Street as their Glasgow terminus. This Daimler Fleetline with Alexander body lays over with a Leyland Titan behind.*

*Buchanan Bus Station was SBG's main Glasgow terminal so independent operators taking advantage of the freedom that deregulation offered chose to use an adjacent plot of open land with basic facilities. A Stagecoach Neoplan Skyliner and Duple and Plaxton-bodied Volvos load on what was fortunately a dry day in April 1985.*

centre and, as the tram fleet dwindled the buses became more visible. But unlike today, when most out-of-town buses conveniently terminate at Buchanan Bus Station, the Scottish Bus Group's vehicles were bewilderingly spread over several bus stations and other on-street termini. Green Scottish Omnibuses types were easy to find as I would often arrive in Glasgow in one. They used Buchanan Street bus station, known by blue Alexander buses as Killermont Street bus station. Alexander's associated red-painted David Lawson routes used nearby Dundas Street bus station. Red Central SMT buses used Killermont Street and Waterloo

Street stations, while red Western SMT buses used Waterloo Street and stances on Clyde Street, which as you might expect was right by the River Clyde. Confused? I was at first until I had worked out where these places were, but of course I managed with the determination of a true bus spotter.

### Working in Glasgow

Express coach deregulation in 1980 persuaded some established operators to start competitive

*The view from the writer's window in the office block at Buchanan Bus Station was an understandable distraction. In April 1985, the pre-deregulation scene includes blue Midland, green Eastern, red Central and Western and blue and yellow Citylink vehicles. Typical Glasgow tower blocks loom in the background.*

ABOVE: *Variety on Glasgow's Argyle Street in September 1986, with a constant line of competing buses – from right a Strathclyde Leyland Atlantean/Alexander, a new Central Scottish Alexander-bodied Leyland Olympian, a Kelvin Scottish ex-London AEC Routemaster, a Central Leyland Leopard/Alexander and in the background a Strathclyde Marshall-bodied Volvo Ailsa and a Kelvin Metrobus.*

BELOW: *Scottish Bus Group's Clydeside and Kelvin companies invested in ex-London Routemasters to compete in Glasgow. When this photo was taken in June 1992, Kelvin had been merged with Central Scottish to create Kelvin Central Buses. This apparently unregistered Routemaster is EDS 98A, formerly 6 CLT, operating on the long 5A route from Clydebank.* GAVIN BOOTH

services throughout Scotland and beyond. Among those encouraged to try their hand at bus and then coach operation were brother and sister Brian Souter and Ann Gloag. These early forays grew into the vast Stagecoach empire, as we now know it.

Years later I would be based in Buchanan Bus Station – the 1977 one – in my marketing role with Scottish Bus Group. I had an office overlooking the concourse so I could watch everything moving in and out, which of course I did, and as this was in 1986, at the time of deregulation of bus services, it was a particularly interesting view. The group had carried out a major reorganisation of its

*SBG was the launch customer for the double-deck MCW Metroliner and here the first departure to London is being piped out of Buchanan Bus Station in March 1983, working for Western Scottish. Pipers were not routinely involved in piping Metroliners out on their journeys.* GAVIN BOOTH

operating companies in 1985 in anticipation of the big challenges that everybody suspected were to come. The largest group companies lost chunks of territory, often reluctantly. Western's Renfrewshire and Inverclyde areas became Clydeside Scottish; Midland lost its south-western area to the new Kelvin Scottish company; Central gained Eastern's Airdrie and Coatbridge operations but lost its Dunbartonshire services to Kelvin.

We launched the new liveries at Buchanan Bus Station in June 1985, though two of them were quickly revised: Kelvin opted for the more eye-catching blue/yellow scheme in place of the original restrained blue/pale blue, and Lowland moved to a darker green to offset its yellow.

Clydeside and Kelvin relied heavily on Glasgow business and adopted a buccaneering approach to the Glasgow market with new services in Strathclyde Buses' heartland, some using ex-London Routemasters with conductors. These were certainly not companies in the traditional SBG mould, and it was exciting working with their energetic managing directors to exploit these new freedoms. They adopted bright liveries – red and yellow for Clydeside and blue and yellow for Kelvin – and worked hard to establish their place in the competitive Glasgow scene. That they ultimately had to retire wounded from high-frequency competition reflected the persistent efforts by Strathclyde Buses to consolidate its position as the principal city operator. By the time SBG faced privatisation, Kelvin had been incorporated into Central Scottish and Clydeside back into Western in preparation for the forthcoming sell-off. Although initially five SBG companies were sold

*First has transferred buses from its other UK companies into the Glasgow fleet. This 1994 Volvo Olympian (above), seen in Union Street in 2009, started life with First Bristol. The 1991 Volvo Citybus (below) was new to Greater Manchester Buses. Both vehicles had Northern Counties bodies.*

to management-led employee buy-outs, including Kelvin Central and Western, within a few years these companies had passed into new ownership: Kelvin Central to Strathclyde Buses, and Western, now separated again from Clydeside, to Stagecoach, while Clydeside went to the emerging British Bus.

*In 2009 First Glasgow bought 25 12m-long three-axle ADL Enviro500 82-seaters. This one is seen in Renfield Street when new. These have now all passed to First Aberdeen.*

*First Glasgow uses colourful branding on main corridors. The 38 wears this blue-green colour, seen on a 2019 ADL Enviro400.*

### Dramatic Change

Glasgow is good at big events; I must reluctantly admit. It hosted the Empire Exhibition in 1938 – before my time, in spite of what Stewart might suggest – and 50 years later, from April to September 1988, it mounted the third Garden Festival in the UK on a 120-acre site on the south bank of the River Clyde. From a transport perspective, and certainly from this Edinburgh son's point of view, an important element (maybe the important element) was the tramway operated by three Glasgow cars, a Blackpool car and – hurrah – Edinburgh tram 35.

In the 60-odd years that I have known Glasgow it has changed dramatically, and mostly for the better. It is still by far the largest city in Scotland, with a population of around 600,000; but 80 years ago, it was double that. In the meantime, Edinburgh has been catching up, growing to nearly 500,000 and it is estimated our population could overtake Glasgow's by 2032. Mind you, that's an Edinburgh estimate.

I have watched Glasgow shake off its image as a tough, even dangerous place, and recognise and build on its strengths. It has more than 90 public parks and gardens ('Glasgow' is derived from the Gaelic Glaschu, meaning a Dear Green Place); there are wonderful art galleries and museums – including of course the Riverside Museum – and Glasgow has embraced the Victorian and Edwardian splendour of its city centre buildings. And it has a proper big river, the Clyde, flowing through the centre, just like London, Paris, Rome and Budapest and other European capitals – but sadly not Edinburgh.

Glasgow recognises its transport heritage and at the time of the closure of the tramway system in 1962 it held on to a fine selection of older cars that were restored to reflect the colourful liveries of the past. For a number of years these were displayed in a Transport Museum in a section of the Kelvin Hall, alongside a few buses, a fine selection of Scottish locomotives, plus Scottish-built cars and ship models that reflected the city's industrial and maritime past. Now many of these can be seen at the new purpose-built Riverside Museum – in slightly more cramped conditions, perhaps; in Edinburgh, sadly, we can offer nothing similar.

*In 2019 First Glasgow painted three buses in heritage liveries to celebrate 125 years of public transport in the city. This Wright-bodied Volvo B9TL wears Glasgow Corporation's 1959 livery as it heads down Renfield Street.*

## Colourful Buses

One of the joys of walking down into George Square from Queen Street railway station or Buchanan Bus Station has always been the colours of the buses. Glasgow Corporation's green/yellow/cream gave way to Greater Glasgow's variations on a similar theme and then Strathclyde's bright all-over orange – sorry, 'Strathclyde Red'. Then came an uninspiring all-over red, and First's various corporate schemes – Barbie, Barbie 2, then the rather insipid lilac scheme to the latest incarnation that allows a bit more individuality, including colourful route branding, something First Glasgow has embraced enthusiastically. Some colour combinations work better than others, it must be said, but there is certainly no danger that you will miss them in the mean streets of Glasgow.

And it still offers a colourful selection of buses and coaches. Big three-axle Stagecoach and Park's single-deckers and double-deckers on interurban work; the two most prominent independent local operators, Glasgow Citybus and McGill's; and of course, today's dominant force, First Glasgow. Although it was by far the major city operator it was largely indistinguishable from First fleets around the country, with largely standard types in First's largely standard liveries, as well as hand-me-downs from other parts of the empire. But the recent route branding has brightened up the city and established more individuality and there has been substantial investment in new buses.

If there is a downside to Glasgow today it's the urban motorway network that cuts swathes across the city, but in fairness it certainly can speed up the drive into, across and, for Edinburghers, escaping out of the city. Just joking, Stewart.

*Greenock-based McGill's acquired Arriva's Scottish outpost in March 2012 and is now well established as one of the largest bus operators in Scotland. In Union Street in 2019 are a 2007 ex-Arriva Volvo B7RLE/Wright and a 2015 ADL Enviro200.*

# A tale of two cities: Edinburgh

## Glasgow's Miles Better

*This Edinburgh Corporation Alexander-bodied Titan is broadly similar to the Glasgow bus illustrated in the previous chapter, but what a difference Edinburgh's restrained livery makes.*

ALL PHOTOGRAPHS BY THE AUTHOR

Who would write an article about Edinburgh without mentioning the city in the headline? A Glaswegian, of course. **Stewart J Brown** looks at buses in the Scottish capital.

The title is not actually my choice of words, but a promotional slogan coined by Glasgow City Council in the early 1980s. Not, of course, that I would disagree with it. If Glasgow City Council said it, it must be true.

My good friend Edinburgher Gavin Booth nicely captured the alleged differences between Scotland's two biggest cities in the preceding pages. Edinburgh was built on business and banking, in the days when banking was a respectable profession and bank managers were held in awe. Glasgow was built on industry; no planes, but plenty of boats and trains - and trucks and buses, too. All dirty, oily, things. So, there were, and still are, real differences between the two cities even in this post-industrial world. Edinburgh, polite and reserved. Glasgow, friendly and just a wee bit rough around the edges.

Edinburgh has a proper castle. It also has a New Town... built some 200 years ago. And a ludicrously expensive tram line. Glasgow has the remains of a rather more modest castle (at Crookston). And it has New Towns (plural, you will note) built in the 20th century to relieve overcrowding. The nearest is East Kilbride. And Glasgow, as Gavin has already hinted, had one of the finest tramway systems in Europe. But that is a distant memory.

*More typical of Edinburgh's Leyland Titans is this 1956 bus with Metro-Cammell Orion body. There were 300 of these buses weighing around 6.75 tons, a remarkably low weight for a 63-seat double-decker.*

But that is enough about Scotland's greatest city. Let me turn to Edinburgh.

### Smart and Sombre

What impresses any enthusiast visiting Edinburgh is how smart the city's buses are. And it has always been so. The livery of white and maroon

*The railings to the right of the Scottish Omnibuses Bristol Lodekka in St Andrew Square bus station are at the top of the stairs leading down to the subway - a tunnel connecting the island platforms.*

ABOVE: *A 1958 AEC Reliance with Park Royal body from the Scottish Omnibuses fleet has just left Edinburgh bus station on its way to Linlithgow. The Eastern Scottish fleet name had been adopted in 1964.*

*Princes Street is a bus photographer's paradise. In this 1980 view an elderly Bristol Lodekka FS6G heads for Glasgow on the slow service via Salsburgh. No one would have made the end-to-end journey, which took almost two-and-a-half hours.*

*Edinburgh's 1970s standard bus was the Leyland Atlantean with panoramic-windowed Alexander body. In this post-deregulation view a Lothian Atlantean is pursued by an Eastern Scottish ex-South Yorkshire PTE Ailsa.*

(madder, they call it in Edinburgh) is sombre and respectable, a bit like the city itself. By contrast Glasgow's buses have generally been colourful and, sad to relate, often quite scruffy.

When I first went to Edinburgh in the 1960s the Corporation fleet was made up largely of Leyland Titans with utilitarian Metro-Cammell Orion bodies. Now the newest buses in the fleet are impressive Volvo B8Ls with ADL Enviro400LXB bodies finished to a specification which could fairly be described as luxurious. They are probably the most well-specified urban buses in the UK.

There have been flashes of inspirational design in the past. In 1965 Edinburgh pioneered the use of panoramic windows in double-deck buses with an Alexander-bodied Leyland Atlantean in which alternate window pillar sections had been removed from the structure to create double-length windows. It looked good, and this style became the city's standard until 1981, when the Atlantean was replaced by the Olympian.

The first Olympians - long-wheelbase models - had ECW bodies, workmanlike but not head-turning. The Alexander R-types which followed were a bit more stylish, but the most attractive of the Olympians were those delivered from 1996 which had Alexander's Royale body. This was a restyled R-type with curved glass windscreens and square-cornered gasket glazing for the side windows.

By this time Edinburgh Corporation Transport had seamlessly changed into Lothian Region Transport. Scottish local government was re-organised in 1975 and there was visible change in

*Small buses were introduced by Eastern Scottish to compete with Lothian. This shows an Alexander-bodied Dodge S56 after the company had been privatised and was trading as SMT, a name last used in 1964.*

Scotland's other cities' buses. Dundee's turned from drab green to bright blue. In Glasgow, the PTE had a bright new version of the city's established yellow and green. In Aberdeen, the city bus fleet used less green and added a band of salmon pink relief. But it is doubtful if many Edinburgh bus users noticed the transition from ECT to LRT. Same buses; same livery.

Also, by this time Volvo had bought Leyland Bus, in 1988. Lothian continued buying Olympians, Leyland-badged until 1993, and then the upgraded Volvo version from 1994. But with the switch to low-floor models in 1999 Lothian's initial choice was the Dennis Trident. By 2004 there were almost 200 Tridents in service, most with Plaxton President bodies.

In 2005 Lothian reverted to Volvo, buying B7TLs with Wright bodies. Then followed B9TLs, B5TLs and even a few B5LHs - 507 in total - all bodied by Wright. To these have been added 75 second-hand examples, most of which have been refurbished ex-London buses.

Edinburgh Corporation - and Scotland's three other municipal fleets - had adopted the two-door layout for its buses when one-man-operation was introduced at the end of the 1960s. The others abandoned the concept in the mid-1970s or early 1980s, but Lothian persevered, taking two-door

buses right up to 2002. The use of a separate exit door was re-introduced to the city fleet with the triaxle Volvo B8Ls in 2019. These were 100-seaters and it was felt necessary to have two doors to reduce the time spent at busy bus stops.

There was one big change in image, with the adoption of what became known as the harlequin livery, introduced in 1999 to identify low-floor buses. This acknowledged the heritage of the fleet's white and maroon (madder, if you insist) but with a lot more white, a minimum amount of madder, and a pattern of red and gold diamonds. Red and gold diamonds? On a bus? What must the good matrons of Morningside have thought?

Anyway, after a brief period of letting its hair down, Lothian Buses - as the operation had by then become - reverted to maroon and white in 2010, at which time all of the buses in the fleet offered step-free access. Apart from London, it makes

*The Atlanteans in the Lothian fleet were followed by Olympians, the final examples being Volvos with Alexander Royale bodies.*

ABOVE LEFT: *What was known as the harlequin livery brought a bright new look to Edinburgh's streets, as illustrated by a Lothian Buses Volvo B7TL with Plaxton President body, delivered in 2000 and photographed in 2010.*

ABPVE CENTRE: *After the harlequin interlude, Lothian Buses reverted to its traditional livery, but applied in a more modern style. A 2014 Volvo B5TL with Wright body shows the effect as it loads in Princes Street in 2015. It is a Gemini 3 with shallow upper deck windows and a glazed panel alongside the stairs.*

ABOVE RIGHT: *Who could fail to be impressed by Lothian's three-axle Volvo B8Ls with Alexander bodywork? Seen soon after entering service in 2019, this bus loads outside what had been the offices of The Scotsman newspaper from 1905 until 2001 when it became a hotel.*

Edinburgh the only British city where the buses are in broadly the same colours (or in London, colour, singular) as they were 50 years ago.

### The Edinburgh Subway?

In the days before local bus deregulation, Glasgow was served by a multiplicity of Scottish Bus Group companies, adding colour to the city's streets. Edinburgh in effect had but one, Scottish Omnibuses, with guest appearances by Alexander Midland from the west and Alexander Fife from the north. But most departures from the city's bus station in St Andrew Square were green buses operated by Scottish Omnibuses, trading as Eastern Scottish. The green had once been a bright shade but had changed to a darker colour in 1964. Less attractive but, apparently, more durable.

The bus station had opened in 1957 and had four parallel platforms which were connected by

tunnels to stop pedestrians from walking in front of the buses. Quaint. I cannot remember ever using them. Glaswegian pedestrians, who have scant regard for traffic lights, would never have put up with any tunnel nonsense in their bus stations. Perhaps Edinburghers were better behaved. To further confuse Glaswegians, a stern warning in the Eastern Scottish timetable read: "Passengers joining or leaving any platform in this station must use the subway". In Glasgow, the Subway was an underground railway, not a little tunnel. Unless, of course, Edinburgh really did have a Subway and I just never found it. And I am not talking about sandwich shops.

There is still a bus station in Edinburgh. But where Glasgow's Buchanan bus station retains a sense of importance and activity over 40 years after it opened, that in Edinburgh, still with access from St Andrew Square, hides apologetically behind a Louis Vuitton shop. Expensive shop alongside inexpensive bus travel: is this postmodern irony?

SBG-owned Eastern Scottish operated a fairly standardised fleet. The double-deckers were Bristol Lodekkas, succeeded by Daimler Fleetlines and then Leyland Olympians. The single-deckers were AEC Reliances in the main which were followed by Bristol RE and LH models, then Leyland Leopards and Seddon Pennines. Where the Edinburgh municipal fleet was smart; the Eastern Scottish fleet was average (but noticeably better in Edinburgh than it was in Glasgow).

Eastern Scottish took the opportunity of deregulation in 1986 to attack Lothian's routes with high-frequency minibus services. Few small operators tried to run buses in the city. And

There have been other three-axle buses serving Edinburgh. In 2004 Stagecoach Fife took eight triaxle Scania K270UB6 OmniLinks with 56 dual-purpose seats, an old Scottish tradition. They were used on services linking Fife with the capital.

LEFT: *In 2005 First took delivery of 30 Scania/East Lancs OmniDekkas, of which 24 were allocated to its Scottish operations. One heads west along Princes Street in 2005, bound for Bathgate.*

whatever short-term gains the company might have made, what remains of Eastern Scottish is now part of First Bus, and a shadow of its former self. In its heyday the company's Edinburgh depot in New Street was one of the biggest in Scotland with an allocation of 270 buses and coaches. Today, First does not have a depot in the city; the nearest is at Livingston, 18 miles to the west. In recent years, the company has cut back dramatically in and around Edinburgh and the Borders.

*First Scotland East had over 40 Wright StreetLites delivered in 2014-15. The two-tone blue livery has echoes of Alexander Midland, but looks a bit drab on dull days. The sun shines on Princes Street and on a StreetLite with Pioneering Spirit branding for a service linking Edinburgh and West Lothian. This is a 2017 view.*

There have been two main beneficiaries of First's retrenchment. One is Borders Buses, which now runs regular services between Edinburgh and towns such as Melrose, Galashiels and Jedburgh, all once part of Eastern Scottish territory. Borders Buses is owned by West Coast Motors. The other is Lothian which runs two green-liveried fleets. East Coast Buses operates east towards North Berwick and Dunbar; Lothian Country runs west towards Queensferry and Bathgate.

Of the First services which do run in to Edinburgh, many are in a blue livery which is a faint echo of the colours used by Alexander Midland many years ago, but the general effect is drab. Wright StreetLites feature, a type once also seen with First Glasgow but now departed.

Buses in Edinburgh run to strange places. I had heard of Joppa because it is in the Bible. But

Oxgangs? Dumbiedykes? Gorgie (which I do not know how to pronounce - does it have a hard or a soft g in the middle?). Or, perhaps to prove that the good citizens of Edinburgh have a sense of humour, Portobello, which sounds like Porto Bello, an imagined romantic spot on the Algarve coast.

### Ideal for the Lazy

Bus spotting was easy in Edinburgh. Every bus route used Princes Street. Well, that is not quite true, but it is how it seemed. Stand near Waverley Bridge and most types of buses serving the city would pass. And it is as true in 2020 as it was in the past. George Street, Queen Street and St Andrew Square were interesting, too - and all within a few hundred yards of each other. You didn't need to wear out too much shoe leather looking for buses in Edinburgh.

Where Edinburgh does beat Glasgow hands down is tourism. According to Visit Scotland, nine of the country's Top 20 tourist attractions are in Edinburgh, compared with just five in Glasgow. Consequently, city tours are big business with Lothian Buses in the lead, operating purpose-built open toppers in a variety of liveries on a range of urban tours. The company also offers day tours to other parts of Scotland through its Lothian Motorcoaches subsidiary, formed in 2018. The city

*Single-deckers have always been in a minority in the Edinburgh city bus fleet. In 2014 Lothian Buses took 50 Volvo 7900H hybrid buses, making it the biggest UK user of the type.*

*Borders Buses has taken over much of First's operations in the Scottish Borders region. This 2013 Volvo B7RLE was new to Whitelaw of Stonehouse and is seen soon after it was acquired by Borders in 2017.*

tours have faced competition from time to time, most recently with the launch of Bright Bus Tours by First in 2019, using an orange and purple livery which reminds me of the wrapper of a Cadbury's Double Decker, the chocolate bar of choice for the discerning bus enthusiast. Other chocolate bars are available.

The over-riding sense of public transport in Edinburgh, as viewed by an outsider, is one of continuity and stability. It is almost as if deregulation had never happened. Clean, modern, buses in a unified livery, run by a council-owned company, create the sense of a stable network. With plenty of buses running along Princes Street there is a feeling of reliability. There is always a bus approaching, even if it is going to Dumbiedykes when you would rather visit Oxgangs.

I have not been to either. Perhaps they should be on my list of things to do in Edinburgh after I have visited these nine top tourist attractions...

*New for East Coast Buses in 2017 were 15 Volvo B8RLEs with Wright Eclipse Urban 3 bodies. There are almost 50 buses in the East Coast fleet.*

# Brits Abroad 2

ABOVE: *An ADL Enviro500 operating with Tower Transit in the city's financial district. It was new in 2014 to SMRT which took 201 Enviro500s in 2014-15. On green-liveried buses the operator's logo is displayed to the rear of the front wheel and on the front panel.*

*Buses leaving the Pasir Ris interchange, in the northeast of the island, showing the two main types operated. In the lead is a 2015 Volvo B9TL with 82-seat Wright Gemini body. It is followed by a Mercedes-Benz Citaro. Both buses are operated by Go-Ahead Singapore.*

# Going green in Singapore

New operators and a new livery are changing the image of Singapore's bus services. **Colin Douglas** illustrates a selection of current vehicles.

The main island of Singapore measures only 26 miles by 14 yet is home to nearly six million residents. This compares with Greater London at some 32 miles by 24 and a population of over eight million. The island is located 60 miles north of the equator, between Malaysia and Indonesia, and is tropical in nature with high humidity. Air-conditioning in all public transport and buildings makes life bearable.

Singapore was a British trading post and then a colony from about 1820. It regained its independence in 1965 with an ambitious plan to become an economic power in Asia. This has been realised in the years since with vast expansion of jobs, infrastructure, housing, and public transport systems.

In view of the space constraints, the use of the private car is discouraged with huge taxes on buying and running them. Public transport alternatives are some of the best in the world with its extensive Mass Rapid Transport rail network and complementary bus network, all linked together with a series of interchanges

LEFT: *The old SBS Transit livery on a 2012 Wright-bodied B9TL. The rear-view mirrors on Singapore buses carry a yellow triangle to warn pedestrians and cyclists to stay clear. Between 2010 and 2017 SBS Transit bought almost 1,400 Wright-bodied Volvos.*

BELOW: *Still in SMRT livery is another of the large batch of Enviro500s delivered in 2014-15, loading in Selegie Road as it heads to Little India and beyond. These buses are 84-seaters.*

and stations. Five interlinked rail lines are operated, underground in the city centre and on the surface in the suburbs, with around 130 stations. Some 5,800 buses in total are operated on public services. Smartcard technology is to the fore with a whole range of contactless payment cards available for travel on the main systems.

Following some mergers, two companies were formed from 2001 to operate the trains and buses under licence, namely SBS Transit and SMRT, but the government is now moving away from this model for trains and buses, with packages of routes being put out to commercial tender. To facilitate this, all the rail and bus assets of SBS Transit and SMRT were taken over by the government in 2016. The government's Land Transport Authority will retain ownership of the trains and buses, garages and stations and the operator will be paid for running the services, with all fare income being returned to the LTA. This system will be introduced across the entire bus network from 2021 for SBS Transit, and from 2026 for SMRT. In a similar way, this model is to be introduced for the rail system, also operated by SBS Transit and SMRT.

The initial batches of services awarded under competitive tendering went to Tower Transit and to the Go-Ahead group in 2016, with work for around 360 buses each. Go-Ahead Singapore was established and operates out of the new, purpose-built Loyang garage complex in the northeast of the island and from three main transport interchanges. It provides a mix of local and trunk services to the centre of Singapore. Several additional services have since been added which has brought the Go-Ahead Singapore fleet up to about 430 buses. The work previously was undertaken by SBS Transit. Tower Transit, the Australian company familiar in the UK through its operations in London, similarly took over routes from SMRT.

British-made buses have long been popular in Singapore and more so since the introduction of two-door triaxle double-deckers fitted with air conditioning. In the 2000s, Alexander Royale-bodied Volvo Super Olympians were the mainstay of the fleets, being replaced from 2010 onwards by a huge fleet of Wright Eclipse Gemini 2- bodied Volvo B9TLs, their total reaching 1,606 by the end of this model's production in 2017. Most were supplied in kit form to be assembled locally.

Alexander Dennis buses were bought in 2014 with a total of 216 Enviro500s for SMRT, with some later passing to Tower Transit. These are complemented

ABOVE: *This 2006 Volvo B9TL has bodywork by ComfortDelGro Engineering. It is operated by SBS Transit.*

RIGHT: *MAN made some inroads into the Singapore bus market in 2017-18. This Lion's City ND323F with distinctive Malaysian Gemilang body is operated by SBS Transit.*

by other double-deck Volvo and MAN buses fitted with Malaysian Gemilang, Singaporean ComfortDelGro and Australian Volgren bodies, and large numbers of Mercedes-Benz Citaros and various Volvo and MAN single-deckers.

New Alexander Dennis buses are set to return to return in 2020 with an order for 50 twin-staircase, three-door Enviro500 double-deckers fitted with energy-saving drive systems.

A public consultation exercise was held in 2016 to choose a new single colour scheme for the bus fleet, with a choice between red and green. A greater number of the public favoured green and hence the lush green scheme was adopted. It was agreed to paint all the buses being transferred to Tower Transit and Go-Ahead Singapore in this green scheme before they commenced operations. Since then, all new buses for all four operating companies have been supplied in green. Older buses with SBS Transit and SMRT are now starting to appear in the new colour.

TIONG BAHRU RD
> TOA PAYOH INT

145

SBS Transit

SG❤BUS

MAN

SG5992S

# Tramlink odyssey

The far reaches of south London's Tramlink network were a closed book to **Peter Rowlands**. Then one sunny day in 2019 he decided to find out what buses operated there.

n normal times, nearly 30 million people travel on London's Tramlink network every year, and most of them probably do so on a regular basis.

I am not one of them. I live near central London, and the only time I normally use the Tramlink system is for the occasional journey between Wimbledon, its most westerly point, and Croydon, at its heart. So, until 2019 the rest of the Tramlink network – those three tentacles stretching northeast from Croydon to Elmers End and Beckenham and southeast to New Addington – remained a mystery to me. What were they like? What would I find at the end of the lines? And what buses and bus services were operating there?

Tramlink opened in 2000. It was intended to improve social and commercial links in an area of

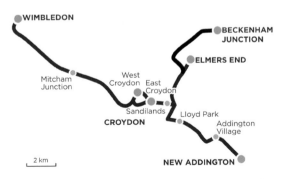

Greater London where there was no underground network. It was built under a private finance initiative, and was originally called Croydon Tramlink, but it was taken over by Transport for London in 2007 and renamed simply Tramlink.

ALL PHOTOGRAPHS BY THE AUTHOR.

LEFT: *This Volvo B5LH of Go-Ahead London General in Wimbledon carries the second generation of Wright's Eclipse Gemini bodywork.*

RIGHT: *More than 50 of these smart Alexander Dennis Enviro400s were delivered to London General in 2008-09 with Optare Olympus bodywork – a rare body/chassis combination. This one is leaving Wimbledon to head north for Putney Bridge.*

It is operated by FirstGroup, but the green and blue livery owes nothing to the group's corporate identity. Prior to 2008 the colour scheme was predominantly red, although FirstGroup's 'Barbie' livery did make an appearance on one tram, and there were also all-over advertising liveries.

The first two dozen articulated trams were built by Bombardier in Austria, but a further dozen were built later by Swiss manufacturer Stadler Rail, and have a slightly more curvy, modern look.

Much of the route runs on former railway alignments, which explains why it strikes out across country at various points where you might imagine it would focus more squarely on local population centres. However, there is a significant amount of street running in Croydon – conjuring up a sense of tramway systems of the past.

My odyssey starts at Wimbledon, which – with a population of around 68,000 – is the second-largest settlement on the network. Tramlink runs into the mainline station here without touching the streets, connecting with National Rail services, and with London Underground's District line.

In the bustling town centre, you will see buses on several significant double-decker trunk services – for instance, the 93 between Putney and North Cheam, the 156 between Wimbledon and Vauxhall, and the 131 between Tooting and Kingston. There are also some more localised single-decker services, including the strange 163, whose meandering route follows three sides of a square to travel between Wimbledon and Morden, taking about eight miles to cover a straight-line distance of fewer than three.

From Wimbledon station, Tramlink strikes out on a dedicated southeasterly alignment. The almost

*Westbound trams pass through the busy West Croydon station on a one-way system, where this Wright StreetLite DF (Door Forward) of Arriva is seen.*

ABOVE: *With only one doorway and a large luggage rack, this Go-Ahead Volvo B9TL with Wright Eclipse Gemini 2 bodywork is one of a batch transferred from East London to operate the limited-stop X26 service from Croydon to Heathrow airport – at over 23 miles, London's longest daytime red bus route.*

ABOVE: *The Optare Esteem was the single-deck version of the company's angular Olympus body, and is seen here in Croydon on an ADL Enviro200 of Go-Ahead.*

ABOVE: *This all-electric Optare MetroCity EV is one of nine delivered to Arriva London in 2014-15. Despite the space taken up by the centre doors, it seats 29 people. This is George Street on the approach to East Croydon Station. The tram tracks are to the right of the bus.*

dead-straight eight-mile stretch between here and Croydon follows the path of the former Wimbledon & Croydon Railway. On a sunny day it is a pretty, leafy trip, though perhaps lacking in variety. If you are a tram enthusiast, however, you will probably be intrigued by the single-track sections with passing places.

At Croydon an abrupt left turn takes us on to public roads and into the town centre, where a one-way system allows eastbound trams to serve West Croydon station, with its small but busy bus station, in addition to the bigger East Croydon station.

With a population of nearly 200,000, the town of Croydon is as big as many cities, and as you would expect, throngs with bus routes serving many destinations: the 60 to Streatham, 154 to Morden, the 264 to Tooting ... the list goes on. The 466 is an oddity; it connects Croydon with Addington village, east of the town, following roughly the same route as the tram system; but it stops short of nearby New Addington, avoiding outright duplication of the tramway service.

East Croydon station is the hub of the tram system. Three tram tracks pass the station frontage, where a suspended white tubular portico partially shelters travellers from the elements. There is also a modest bus station here, with two parallel lanes.

Heading east out of Croydon, the tramway runs for over three quarters of a mile along Addiscombe Road. In some ways this is the most intriguing part of the whole network, providing a compelling reminder of suburban street running by the tramways of the past. Daytime access to private cars is limited, but buses and other traffic share the space with the trams. No overtaking is allowed, which means that when a bus or tram stops, so does all the traffic behind it.

Bus routes using this stretch include the 119 (Croydon Airport to Bromley), the 194 (West Croydon to Lower Sydenham via Crystal Palace), and the 198 (Thornton Heath to Shrublands) – plus of course the 466 to Addington village.

Eventually the tramway crosses Addiscombe Road and shifts on to a dedicated track alongside it. Then a few hundred yards further on, just after a stop named Sandilands, it swings away from the road altogether. A short way further on comes the first fork in the route: north to Elmers End and Beckenham Junction, south to New Addington.

Until exploring this section of the system I had imagined there would be much more suburban street running, but it turns out that all three

A Wright-bodied Volvo
B5LH of Go-Ahead passes
the Cricketers pub on the
Addiscombe Road tram
route out of Croydon. The bus
has the Metrobus fleet name in small
letters integrated into the Go-Ahead London name on the front panel.

branches east of Croydon have a remarkably rural air. Heading north, the scenery is a real surprise. Somehow avoiding London's urban sprawl, the tramway immediately feels as if it is running through open countryside. The landscape is trees, fields, and the occasional farm.

After four more tram stops, the Beckenham Junction branch forks off to the left, but continuing straight on takes us along a short spur to the terminus at Elmers End – an unpretentious commuter town with a mix of high rise and mock Tudor architecture and a triangular village green.

Alexander Dennis Enviro400s and MMC double-deckers both crop up here on the long trunk route 54 between Elmers End and Woolwich, and before long I encounter a relatively rare sight in London these days - Mercedes-Benz Citaros, which Go-Ahead uses for the long, meandering service 358 between Crystal Palace and Orpington. These are to the later design, with pronounced visual 'haunches' over the wheel arches.

Short-wheelbase Enviro200s are also regular performers here. Abellio uses them on the 367 between Croydon and Bromley, while Stagecoach uses them on the 356 between Sydenham and Wickham Row, just outside West Wickham.

Taking a tram back to Arena, the stop prior to the point where the Elmers End spur branches off, I pick up the next one bound for Beckenham

Tramlink leaves public roads for dedicated track where Chepstow Road joins Addiscombe Road, east of Croydon. This is one of the original Bombardier trams.

Flashback to 2000: a single tram on the network was painted in full FirstGroup livery. The rest were originally red and cream, but all were repainted green, blue, and white in 2008-09.

ABOVE: *Dating from 2015, a Go-Ahead London Mercedes-Benz Citaro with its wheel-arch 'haunches' heads past the green at Elmers End on the way from Orpington to Crystal Palace.*

RIGHT: *Short-wheelbase 24-seat single-door ADL Enviro200s with MMC-style bodywork are used by Abellio on the meandering 11-mile route 367 between Croydon and Bromley. This one is seen at Elmers End.*

Junction. Rural scenery again marks much of this section, which briefly heads north-west, then swings north-east on the old Crystal Palace line. Five stations on, we are entering Beckenham Junction station alongside the National Rail line to central London.

Beckenham has a delightful country town aura. Our old friend service 54 reappears here, where it is joined by several new services. Among them is the 227, a single-deck route running east-west between Bromley and Crystal Palace. During my visit Mercedes-Benz Citaros were running on this service, though Stagecoach had lost the route under competitive tendering, and a few weeks later London General took over with smaller Wright StreetLites.

The last branch to explore is the one to New Addington, which involves retracing my steps

over nine stations to Sandilands to head off on a southeastern trajectory. It seems I have picked the wrong day for this exercise; the first two trams towards New Addington are packed to the limit, and there is absolutely no prospect of boarding. I decide to try my luck with the third, but only succeed by sheer determination and a few frowns from those who must squeeze aside to make space for me.

It turns out that there is a pop concert at Lloyd Park, the first stop on the New Addington branch, and to my relief, almost everyone on the tram disembarks there.

This branch of the system is different from the others; the largely dedicated track has been laid specifically for this purpose, mostly alongside existing roads. Again, it is a largely rural route. Even the bus interchange outside the original Addington village is surrounded by greenery. The village itself is a brisk walk further on.

Here the tramway turns southward to run down the side of a main road called Lodge Lane; and before long it enters what feels like another

*An ADL Enviro400 MMC operated by Stagecoach London passes the Elm Tree pub as its sets off from Elmers End on the 10-mile run to Woolwich.*

world. New Addington (population 10,000) was conceived in the 1930s as an overspill town for Croydon, then was expanded after the war. Architecturally it resembles many housing estates closer to London, being made up of a mix of semi-detached houses and flats with a strong 1930s and 1950s feel; but the place seems to have been magically dropped intact into a rural setting. It is not part of a larger town; it is complete and of itself and is surrounded by countryside. Only two roads run in and out of it, and the one to the south merely links to relatively minor roads in that area.

However, in addition to trams it is relatively well served by buses. There is a high-profile double-deck service, the 64, which runs north to Thornton Heath Pond, and there are three single-deck services. One of these, the 130, also heads north to Thornton Heath, while the 314 goes northeast to Eltham. Just one service, the 464, heads south from the town to Biggin Hill and Tatsfield.

These services all take slightly different but equally circuitous routes through the hinterland of the town itself, ensuring that most parts of it are covered. They also all visit the town centre – a place known as the Parade, where the shops have been shoehorned into a long terrace on one side and face on to an open area.

The Tramlink network currently covers 17 route

*A Stagecoach ADL Enviro200 in Beckenham High Street.*

miles altogether. There have been numerous proposals for extensions, and in the early days one of the most plausible would have seen a spur heading northwards from the Beckenham branch to Crystal Palace, just a few miles away. However, that scheme now has very low priority. The plan that looks most likely to come to fruition at the time of writing is arguably more ambitious, extending the Wimbledon branch on a sharp southbound dogleg that would take it all the way to Sutton, around six miles away.

If built, this will introduce intrepid explorers to yet another new world of local buses. But it might be premature to start planning an expedition in the hope of finding trams there any time soon.

LEFT: *The tree-lined Parkway adds a welcome bucolic touch to the commercial centre of New Addington. This is an ADL Enviro400 of Arriva on the 64 to Thornton Heath.*

BELOW: *Abellio is using long-wheelbase ADL Enviro200 MMCs on route 130, which (like the 64) goes northwards to Thornton Heath.*

# Coaching **rarities**

**Geoff Mills** illustrates some of the less common types of coaches seen on British roads in the last four decades.

LEFT: *Unicar had a go at the British coach market in 1979-80 and achieved 100 sales over the two-year period. Most were on Bedford YMT chassis including this immaculately restored coach which was repatriated from Malta by Paul S Winson of Loughborough. Unicar bodies were built in Spain by Union Carrocera.*

*At first glance this looks like another ungainly midicoach on a Mercedes-Benz light truck chassis. It is in fact a Spanish-built Ebro, a Perkins-engined 7.5-tonne L75 with 23-seat Coachcraft body. It was new in 1985 and is seen three years later with Ruffles of Castle Hedingham.*

MIDDLE LEFT: *Irizar has a significant presence in the UK in the 21st century, but at the start of the 1980s it was a small player. This 1981 coach is an Urko on a Volvo B58 chassis, seen in 2001 in the ownership of C&G Coaches of Chatteris, Cambridgeshire. The split floor level was an unusual feature, reminiscent of an earlier generation of observation coaches. Irizar sold around a dozen coaches in 1980-81.*

*Leyland tried its hand at selling complete integral coaches with the Royal Tiger Doyen. It was launched in 1982. This coach was supplied to Pickup of Rochdale in the spring of 1988 and was one of the last Doyens to enter service. In 2000 it was running for Fourways of Chelmsford. Here at Brooklands it poses alongside an aircraft in a remarkably similar livery.*

BOTTOM LEFT: *Wright of Ballymena made a few attempts to sell coaches but, like most other bus builders, found the coach market a challenge. This boxy-looking vehicle was not Wright's most attractive design. It was on a Bedford SB5 chassis and was supplied to Myalls of Bassingbourn in 1984. Here it is at the 2011 UK Coach Rally in Peterborough.*

*Wadham Stringer dabbled in coaching with a body called the Winchester. This 1995 example is on a MAN 11.190 chassis and is fitted with a wheelchair lift just ahead of the rear axle. It was new to Coles of Eversley in Berkshire and is seen here in 2002 with Felix of Long Melford, Suffolk.*

MIDDLE RIGHT: *Drogmoller was a German manufacturer of integral coaches and it exhibited this unusual coach, the Comet, at the 1984 Motor Show. It was delivered to Bergland of Watford at the start of 1985 and was followed by two more in 1986. This rare coach survives in preservation in the fleet of GH Watts of Leicester.*

BOTTOM RIGHT: *Dennis enjoyed success in the bus market in the early 1980s but fared less well when it came to coaches. Between 1983 and 1988 it sold just 56 Dorchester coaches in the UK, the vast majority going to public sector fleets. This coach was an exception, being new in 1984 to Gastonia of Cranleigh, just ten miles from Dennis's Guildford factory. It has a Duple Caribbean body; both Duple and Dennis were part of the Hestair Group at the time. In 2002 it was running for MD Travel Hire of Ipswich.*

*Dutch builder Van Rooijen tried selling coaches in the UK in the mid-1980s, securing a total of ten sales. Safford's Tours of Little Gransden, Cambridgeshire, bought this Volvo B10M in 1985. The body was known as the Odyssee - the Dutch spelling of odyssey.*

TOP LEFT: *King Long was the first Chinese manufacturer to sell coaches in the UK. This is an XMQ6127, probably the most popular model in Britain and available between 2007 and 2016. It is seen with Lowestoft-based Angie's Tours in 2016. King Long still builds buses and coaches but is no longer active in the UK.*

MIDDLE: *Belgian manufacturer LAG unveiled its DAF-engined EOS integral in 1989 and had a right-hand drive model ready for the UK in the spring of 1990. However, in June 1990 LAG was taken over by Van Hool, and the LAG name quickly disappeared. The Van Hool EOS was sold in Britain throughout the 1990s. This example was new to Hurst's of Wigan in 1993 and is seen ten years later with Towler of Emneth.*

BOTTOM LEFT: *Ayats exhibited this striking coach, the Diana, at the 1982 Motor Show. The concept of a high floor with seats above the driver was novel. The coach had Magirus-Deutz running units. Despite being a rare type in Britain, this Diana was still running in 1997 when it was being operated by M&E Coaches of Shoeburyness, Essex.*

RIGHT: *Turkish manufacturer BMC had some sales successes in the early 2000s. The Probus 850 was a midicoach, typically with 35 seats. Lewis Coaches of Brandon bought this one in 2004. The BMC name reflects the company's origin in 1964 as an assembler of vehicles for the British Motor Corporation.*

TOP RIGHT: *Ayats reappeared in the UK at the start of the new millennium with a range of MAN-powered integral coaches which sold in small numbers. Hamilton of Uxbridge was the biggest customer for the single-deck Atlas, taking three - out of ten imported - in 2002. In 2008 one of the trio was owned by County Coaches of Brentwood.*

MIDDLE: *Beulas started selling coaches in Britain in 1996 - and is still here, so while its products are not as commonplace as, say, Plaxton or Van Hool, it has a reasonable presence on Britain's roads. This is one of the less common Beulas models, the high-capacity Glory with 71 seats. It was new to Florida of Halstead in 2010 and is based on a MAN 24.480 underframe.*

BOTTOM RIGHT: *Autosan is a Polish manufacturer and it sold rather basic coaches in the UK between 2005 and 2010. Many had two-plus-three seating for use as school coaches, including this 67-seat A1012T model of Amber Coaches of Rayleigh. It is one of a pair bought in 2006.*

BELOW: *Noge bodies were first available in the UK in 1998 and were supplied exclusively on MAN underframes. The key model was the Catalan. Sales were handled by dealer Mentor Coach & Bus, and when Mentor closed in 2008 Noge disappeared from the UK, after selling around 200 coaches. Noge closed soon after, a victim of the recession in Spain. This is a 1999 delivery, new to Star of Ossett, West Yorkshire, but here in the fleet of Enigma Travel of Wivenhoe Essex, in 2014.*

# Pole Position

A relatively recent development in the ever-evolving field of photography is the use of camera poles. **John Robinson** finds poles a valuable aid to bus photography.

ALL PHOTOGRAPHS BY THE AUTHOR.

*Ipswich Buses 33 (YR61 RRV), one of 18 Scania OmniCity N230UDs acquired in 2017-18. New to CentreWest as dual-doorway vehicles, the seamless conversion to single-door can be seen as it heads alongside the River Orwell at Wherstead operating service 92 to East Bergholt in October 2019. The Orwell Bridge, opened in 1982 and carrying the A14, dominates the background.*

The big benefit of poles is that they allow cameras to be deployed at heights which would have previously been considered impossible to gain a different perspective on the subject. Whilst poles have been in use with railway photographers for some time, they are still rare in the field of bus photography.

From a practical perspective, pole photography is only feasible with digital cameras, many of which now incorporate Wi-fi. By means of an app, the camera can be controlled remotely from a smartphone or tablet, onto which a live view of the scene can be relayed. However, even before this technology became available, I was taking pole shots, using either modified painter's poles - up to

*Stagecoach East Dennis Trident/Alexander ALX400 18413 (AE06 GZK) crosses Alconbury Bridge in July 2012, the final day of Stagecoach operation of service 46 between Huntingdon and Peterborough. The people in the shot, one of whom I knew, were happy to be strategically placed to improve the composition.*

*Approaching the Fenland village of Turves, situated on the back road between March and Whittlesey, is preserved Grimsby Cleethorpes Transport AEC Bridgemaster 133 (NJV 995), the last of a batch of four new in 1960. Its Park Royal body was converted to open-top by the operator in 1974 and it continued in service until 1981 when it entered preservation. It is seen alongside the Twenty Foot River during the Fenland Running Day on May 15, 2016.*

*Eastern Counties RLE747 (GCL 349N) was the last of a batch of eight Bristol RELHs with ECW bus shell bodywork with coach seating new in 1974. Normally, vehicles of this dual-purpose configuration would have worn red and white NBC local coach livery, but these were finished in full National white coach livery. After a succession of owners, it entered preservation in 2003 and is depicted crossing Beggars Bridge over the Twenty Foot River as it heads back into Whittlesey during the Fenland Running Day on May17, 2014.*

five metres - or extended monopods. The camera shutter was triggered by a wireless remote control. The receiver was attached to the camera's hot-shoe and connected by a short lead to one of the camera's external connection ports whilst the transmitter was held in the hand.

With this rudimentary set up, however, I had no view of the subject being photographed so was effectively shooting blind. Even so, with practice I managed a reasonable success rate. This was achieved by taking a test picture. The image could

then be checked for composition, with adjustments made to the orientation of the pole to frame the shot as required.

Theoretically a film camera could be deployed on a pole using a long cable release, but there would be no way of checking the image until the film was developed so it is likely there would be a high image wastage rate.

However, with Wi-fi, and the ability to see the live view whilst shooting, the shot can be accurately composed. I currently use two cameras for pole

*First Hampshire & Dorset 42513 (R413 WPX) a Plaxton Pointer 2-bodied Dennis Dart SLF, one of a batch of 20 new to FirstBus-owned Southampton Citybus in 1998, meets 66884 (MX55 HHO) a Wright Eclipse Urban-bodied Volvo B7RLE new to First Manchester in 2005. They are seen in August 2013 crossing the Itchen Bridge linking Woolston and Southampton. Opened in 1977, it replaced the Woolston Floating Bridge, a chain ferry, at the same location.*

*Heading along Chester Road, Grappenhall, alongside the Bridgewater Canal in October 2015, operating a service from Lymm High School, is Network Warrington 174 (P324 SWC). It is a 1996 Volvo Olympian with Alexander (Belfast) bodywork which had been new to Dublin Bus. Fortuitously, the narrow boats appeared just before the bus arrived.*

RIGHT: *Taken from the same position on the canal bank this eye-level shot, where the hedge completely blocks the view of the road, amply demonstrates the opportunities that pole photography provides in situations such as this.*

photography; a full-frame Nikon Df, which has no Wi-fi so requires an attachment to provide this functionality, and a mirrorless Fujifilm X-T1 which has an APS-C size sensor and built-in Wi-fi.

The Df is heavier and bulkier than the X-T1, so the biggest lens I tend to use on the Nikon for pole work is the Nikkor 24-85mm short zoom. I have concerns that anything larger could place too much strain on the tripod head screwed into the top of the pole. However, the smaller Fujifilm is less of a problem in this respect and I happily use the Fujifilm 55-200mm zoom lens, which allows a lot more freedom for composing shots.

I now use a Broge photographic pole for most of my pole photography. This is constructed of carbon fibre to minimise weight and incorporates moveable sections which can be extended up to 10 metres; fully contracted, it is about 1.8 metres long. The pole is deployed by standing it on the

ground using an optional footplate to steady it and extending the sections to the desired height. Where possible, to steady it further I support it against signs, walls or railings as standing in the same spot holding it for a protracted period can be quite tiring, especially if the wind is strong.

All my previous poles were deployed by holding them aloft at chest height just before the subject came into frame; with camera, receiver and transmitter all powered up, and the camera settings arranged, pressing the transmitter button fired the shutter.

Using Wi-fi the picture-taking process is quite different as the cameras are operating in 'PC mode' so whatever settings are physically showing on the camera are overridden by the app. This allows the settings to be adjusted through the app before taking the picture. The point of focus can be set simply by tapping the live view image in the desired

ABOVE: *The Wellingborough 100 event was held over the weekend of March 16-17, 2013 to commemorate a centenary of bus services in the Northamptonshire town. Among the vehicles taking part was Stagecoach's ex-Eastern Counties 1966 Bristol Lodekka FLF453 (JAH 553D). Previously painted in standard Stagecoach livery it had returned to Tilling red and cream when seen in Castle Way, Wellingborough.*

BELOW: *Taking part in a road run in connection with the Wellingborough 100 event is this superbly restored Northampton Corporation Daimler CWD6 129 (VV 8934). New in 1945, its Duple bodywork was to 'relaxed' utility specification. It was withdrawn in 1959 and sold for scrap to Hunt's at Molesworth, Huntingdonshire. Remarkably, it managed to survive there for over 30 years before being acquired for preservation in 1991. It is crossing Irthlingborough Viaduct, built in 1936, which carries the A6 over the River Nene.*

*Based in Flitwick and set up at the beginning of 2018, WeberBus introduced a striking blue and black livery. Alexander ALX400-bodied Dennis Trident LX04 FYD, new to East London in 2004, although latterly with Grant Palmer, heads through Radwell on its regular afternoon service 825 from Sharnbrook Academy to Clapham and Oakley in February 2020. Following are two Herberts Travel Volvos, an ex-Dublin Bus B7TL/Alexander ALX400 followed by an Olympian/Alexander which had been new to Selkent. Whilst a perfectly acceptable photograph could have been obtained from the roadside, using the pole to shoot over the hedge has allowed a wider view to be captured.*

position. However, the setting of the focal length if using a zoom lens needs to be done manually before the pole is extended.

Once the images are taken, they are loaded onto the app which takes a second or two each; until completed this process prevents any more photographs from being taken. This can be problematical if, for example, a procession of buses is passing the camera as it is highly likely that not all will be able to be photographed.

*In August 2011, Grant Palmer of Flitwick took on a number of services in north Bedfordshire previously operated by Cedar Travel of Bedford. Plaxton Pointer-bodied Dennis Dart Y857 TGH, new to London Central in 2001, wears the mauve and white Bedford Borough Council livery used on some of the vehicles. It is seen in passing the Church of St Nicholas in the pretty village of Swineshead, heading to Bedford on an early morning service 28 from Kimbolton.*

Wi-fi consumes quite a lot of power, so camera batteries will drain more quickly than would otherwise be the case. It is therefore essential to carry a few fully charged spares and to ensure that the smartphone or tablet are fully charged to prevent photographic sessions being cut short!

Using the Broge pole, with its much greater reach than any of my previous poles, wind becomes one of the biggest problems as the diameters of the retracting poles (of which there are seven) gradually reduce towards the top so the camera is prone to being buffeted. I have noticed on several occasions that even if it is calm at ground level 20 or 30 feet up the wind currents can be quite strong making the pole sway gently. Sharp photos can still be achieved, if a fast shutter speed is selected; I would normally aim to use at least 1/1000 second when possible.

I have discovered two specific situations where the pole can be a useful addition to my photographic arsenal. The first of these is at locations where a perfectly good conventional eye-level shot can already be obtained but by using the pole a higher viewpoint completely transforms the picture. The second is where use of a pole opens angles at locations where a satisfactory (or any) eye-level shot may not be possible. For instance, there might be obstacles such as bollards, railings, walls, or hedges which partially obscure the vehicle if taken at eye-level. Similarly, in the case of the Cambridgeshire Guided Busway for example, parts of the track are on embankments, so the bus is above head height when viewed from the adjacent walkway. However, using the pole to shoot high enables photographs to be taken at these otherwise unsuitable locations.

Use of a pole will, of course, always allow much more of the surroundings to be included in the composition than a conventional shot; this dovetails with my desire to photograph buses in the context of their working environment rather than simply taking a pure technical record shot of the vehicle. A favourite of mine is photographing buses as they cross bridges, with the pole positioned either on or alongside the bridge. Features of interest such as rivers, railways or other roads passing beneath, which would not otherwise appear in the photograph, can therefore be included.

Shooting from high up, the camera is inevitably pointing down slightly, causing any verticals near the camera to converge. These can, however,

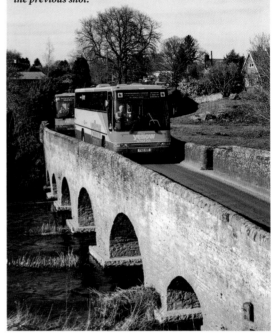

*An earlier generation of Sharnbrook school buses (and pupils) are seen nine years previously in March 2011. Wearing 'big yellow school bus' livery, Plaxton Premiere-bodied Volvo B10Ms 52369 (P169 KBD) and 52482 (R182 DNH), new to Stagecoach United Counties in 1996 and 1997 respectively, cross Radwell bridge over the River Great Ouse. The location is just under half-a-mile before the previous shot.*

BELOW*: Wearing Stagecoach East Midlands' InterConnect livery and operating service 505 from Spalding to King's Lynn, 15614 (OU10 BGF), a Scania N230UD/ADL Enviro400 new to Thames Transit heads east along the A17. It is seen crossing Cross Keys Bridge at Sutton Bridge, Cambridgeshire in March 2020. Opened in 1897, at a cost of £80,000, it was a road-and-rail hydraulic swing bridge crossing the tidal River Nene with the Midland and Great Northern Joint Railway's line from Spalding to King's Lynn using one side and the side the bus is on being used by road traffic. The railway closed to passengers in 1959 and the following year the railway track over the bridge was covered with sleepers to form a second roadway; this was replaced by a permanent carriageway in 1963.*

ABOVE: *Sister vehicle 15616 (OU10 BGO), also in InterConnect livery, passes the unusually named Foul Anchor operating service 50 from Sutton Bridge to Wisbech, also in March 2020. This is one of 11 similar vehicles based at nearby Long Sutton, which are maintained at Skegness depot. Use of the pole has allowed more of the flat landscape of the area to be captured, with the River Nene clearly visible. In the background is the gas-powered Sutton Bridge Power Station.*

ABOVE RIGHT: *Lothian Transport added 67 Alexander Royale-bodied Volvo Olympians to its fleet in 1996-97. After passing through several subsequent operators P423 KSX, formerly Lothian 423, is seen with Herberts Travel, Blunham, Bedfordshire in June 2019. It is seen crossing Felmersham Bridge over the River Great Ouse to take up a school service from Sharnbrook Academy. This was my first outing with the new 10-metre pole although it wasn't necessary to extend it fully for this picture.*

*Apparently devoid of passengers, Stagecoach East 13905 (BU69 XYE), one of 12 ADL Enviro400XLB-bodied Volvo B8Ls for the Cambridgeshire Guided Busway approaches St Ives park-and-ride. It is operating service B from Cambridge to Godmanchester on March 23, 2020 just hours before prime minister Boris Johnson announced the Coronavirus lockdown restrictions.*

be corrected in Photoshop or similar software packages in which verticals can be digitally tilted until they are parallel.

With pole photography there can always be a temptation to shoot with the pole fully extended, but as well as reducing the stability of the camera it can result in the bus roof dominating the picture. For this reason, I tend to photograph single-deckers from a lower height than double-deckers.

On a final and very important note it goes without saying that when deploying the pole it is absolutely essential that the location is assessed first to ensure there are no overhead cables present and, if there are, they are at a sufficiently safe distance to avoid potentially deadly consequences.

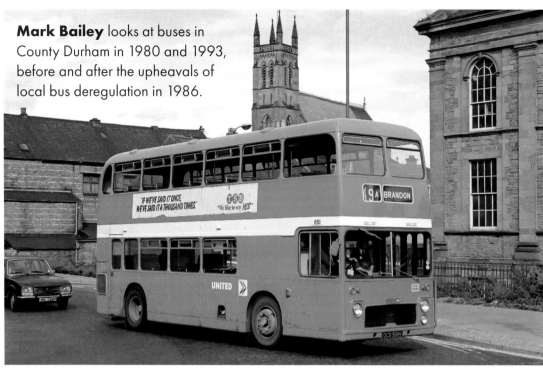

**Mark Bailey** looks at buses in County Durham in 1980 and 1993, before and after the upheavals of local bus deregulation in 1986.

# THE LAND OF THE
## PRINCE BISHOPS

C ounty Durham boasts a rich heritage and a proud place in world history. Named in the style commonplace in Ireland but the only example in Britain, the traditional title of a shire county – Durhamshire – was never formally adopted. For much of the last millennium the area was ruled by the Bishops of Durham with an authority almost on a par with the monarchy, initially from their palace in Durham Castle and latterly from Auckland Castle.

The county benefited from abundant natural resources and the Durham coalfield was one of the most extensive in Britain; at its peak there were 170,000 miners working in hundreds of collieries. The need to transport the coal towards the coast led to the opening of the horse-drawn Tanfield Railway

ABOVE: *In 1973 United acquired 20 ECW-bodied Bristol VRTs from the Scottish Bus Group in exchange for Bristol Lodekkas. Pictured in Durham ready for service 49A to Brandon is conductor-operated ex-Western SMT 651 (OCS 591H).*

LEFT: *Northern General's double-deck fleet was much more varied than United's. Arriving in Bishop Auckland on service 219 from Sunderland is dual-door ECW-bodied Leyland Atlantean 3306 (MPT 306P), sporting an advert promoting the company's coach hire service.*

The oldest vehicles in the Darlington Corporation fleet in June 1980 were Daimler CCG5s with Roe bodywork. Fleet number two (302 VHN) is seen in the town centre on service 2C to Salters Lane on the northern edge of the town.

The largest independent operator in the county in 1980 was Bishop Auckland-based OK Motor Services. Pictured squeezing through the town's busy marketplace on the Evenwood service is Massey-bodied Leyland Titan OVX 143D, which had been new to Colchester Corporation.

ABOVE: The Eden Bus Services was based in West Auckland and operated a modern fleet of Leyland Leopards. Plaxton Derwent-bodied L12 (PPT 445P) is arriving in Bishop Auckland on service 92 from Newton Aycliffe and Shildon.

in 1725, followed 100 years later by the Stockton & Darlington Railway using steam locomotives (manufactured locally in Shildon) to pull trains carrying passengers as well as freight – a pivotal moment heralding railway expansion not only across Britain but the world.

The area around Consett on the edge of the Pennines was also rich in iron ore and limestone, which led to the establishment of a major steelworks along with ancillary industries. Even though many towns and villages had developed in close proximity to the collieries there was still a requirement to transport thousands of people to their workplaces, and the provision of bus services

was a profitable business during the first half of the last century. The decline in coal mining started after World War Two, with the last colliery closing in 1994. British Steel shut its Consett plant in 1980.

The two National Bus Company subsidiaries serving County Durham in 1980 were United Automobile Services and Northern General Transport, with Darlington Transport the sole municipal operator. The accompanying photographs illustrate the variety of operators and vehicles serving the county at two contrasting points in time either side of bus deregulation in 1986, firstly in June 1980 and then again in August 1993.

RIGHT: **Trimdon Motor Services ran an extensive network of routes across the county. Leaving Durham on service 56 to Spennymoor is Duple Dominant-bodied Leyland Leopard MGR 915T. Following deregulation in 1986, subsidiary companies were created to compete in Cleveland and Tyne & Wear, and in 1990 the original TMS was acquired by the Caldaire group and absorbed into United.**

LEFT: **Weardale Motor Services had a double-deck fleet primarily for Wolsingham Grammar School contracts. The company also operated several coaches fitted with three-plus-two bus seating to provide additional capacity at school times. Seen in Bishop Auckland on the main stage service 101 to Crook and Stanhope is 68-seat Plaxton Elite-bodied Volvo B58 GGR 307N.**

LEFT: *Plaxton Highway service buses were popular with several of the northeast independents. Willington-based Bond Bros had several on AEC Reliance chassis such as JPT 790C, pictured in Bishop Auckland working service 108 from its home village.*

RIGHT: *After deregulation, Spennymoor-based Gardiner Bros expanded into bus operation. Pictured in Chester-le-Street is Willowbrook 003-bodied Leyland Leopard TPT 23V working service 734 to Ouston. The coach was new to United but was acquired from Northumbria Motor Services, which had taken over United's Northumberland operations when the company was split in two by NBC in 1986.*

LEFT: *United was privatised in 1987 and by August 1993 had passed from original purchasers Caldaire to the Westcourt group, set up by former Caldaire directors. In 1990 two Leyland Tigers with Alexander (Belfast) Q-type bodywork were bought for evaluation. Number 1235 (H279 LEF) is departing Darlington on service 75 to Barnard Castle and Middleton-in-Teesdale. United would be taken over by Travel West Midlands in 1994, and then sold to Cowie, the forerunner of Arriva, in 1996.*

LEFT: *Long-established independent Gypsy Queen sold out to the Go-Ahead group in 1989 but in August 1993 there was no obvious sign that ownership had changed. Duple 300-bodied Volvo B10M E107 DJR was allocated fleet number 4749 on paper and is captured in its home village of Langley Park working the original service 53 to Durham. It was the first example of Duple's short-lived 300-series bus body.*

RIGHT: *In 1990 Darlington Transport purchased six Daimler Fleetlines from Nottingham sporting that operator's distinctive Northern Counties bodywork. Loading in the town centre on service two to Skerne Park is 206 (PAU 206R). Following intense competition from United and Your Bus and predatory action from Stagecoach-owned Busways, Darlington Transport ceased trading in November 1994.*

LEFT: *Classic Coaches of Annfield Plain commenced competitive bus services in 1992 targeting Go-Ahead routes in particular. Seen leaving Stanley in August 1993 on service 72B to Chester-le-Street is LCY 110X, a Willowbrook 003-bodied Leyland Leopard new to South Wales Transport. The yellow wording beneath the windscreen reads 'Not part of the Northern Group'.*

LEFT: *The Go-Ahead group acquired Shaws Coaches of Craghead in 1992 and retained its identity for a few years. Amongst the vehicles painted in Shaws colours were several Leyland National 2s, as illustrated by 4713 (FTN 713W) in Chester-le-Street arriving on service 729 from Stanley.*

RIGHT: *OK Motor Services embraced bus deregulation in a big way, rebranding itself as OK Travel and expanding its fleet from 70 vehicles to more than 200 in just ten years. Purchases included six new Northern Counties-bodied Leyland Olympians one of which was K109 YVN, a long-wheelbase 82-seater new in 1992. It is seen in Bishop Auckland in August 1993 about to work the 724 service to Newcastle upon Tyne. OK sold out to the Go-Ahead group in March 1995.*

LEFT: *Northern General celebrated its 80th anniversary in 1993 and repainted ten-year-old MCW Metrobus 3509 (UTN 509Y) to publicise this milestone. It is in Langley Park on the X6 service to Sunderland.*

*Midland Classic Routemaster RM1168 is seen here in Hanley, working on hire to RML Travel Burslem on its route 40, Hanley to Birches Head. It was taking part in a running day in 2009 and has been fitted with a complete set of London-style blinds for the occasion.*

**Cliff Beeton** charts the growth of a Midlands independent.

# Fifteen years of
# Midland Classic

Midland Classic was founded in July 2005 by James Boddice with a pair of former Go-Ahead London Central AEC Routemasters, RM 1168 and RM1305. They were originally registered 168 CLT and 305 CLT but had been re-registered 798 UXA and 799 UXA. They were both to be used for a private hire operation based at a yard at Swadlincote in Derbyshire.

Just 11 months later, in June 2006, the company started its first bus service, the 21 linking Swadlincote and Burton on Trent Hospital via Castle Gresley and Linton. It was the long way round between the two towns but had the potential for more passengers. The company continued to expand, mainly by taking on services that had headways reduced or were abandoned by other operators as opposed to direct head-to-head competition. Success at winning council tenders would see further routes added to the portfolio along with various school contracts.

The company introduced a livery of yellow and red. It was based on the final livery used by Midland Red North and Stevensons under British Bus control before the creation of Arriva, and the subsequent adoption of the Arriva Cotswold stone and aquamarine national livery. Some of the early vehicle purchases had previously been operated by Stevensons and Midland Red North, and as a tribute some were restored into Stevensons' original yellow, white and black livery, a practice that continues to this day. The Routemasters, however, never received fleet livery. They remained in London red with a yellow cantrail band and with Midland Classic fleet names in London-style gold and retained their London fleet numbers. RM 1305 left the fleet 12 months later.

Over half of the Midland Classic fleet originates from London, with both double and single-deckers. This echoes the practice at Stevensons, which operated a large fleet of ex-London Transport Fleetlines. The red in the Midland Classic livery is the London Buses shade.

Fleet numbers and timetables are displayed with a London-style Johnson font, and some early double-deck purchases had purpose-made London-style destination blinds fitted until continual changes to the routes made it more cost-effective to replace them with electronic displays.

Interesting early fleet arrivals were an ex-West Midlands PTE Leyland Titan, one of the few delivered new to an operator outside London, and an Alexander-bodied Leyland Lynx, which was new to Ulsterbus and one of the few Lynxes not to be bodied by Leyland. This was a former Stevensons vehicle and was later joined by an early Leyland Lynx which was delivered new to Stevensons. Also arriving were two ex-Greater Manchester Buses MCW Metrobuses from Cotterills of Mitcheldean, one of which had previously operated for Stevensons. All received Midland Classic livery.

Another ex-Stevensons vehicle was prototype Metrobus TOJ 592S, which in early life worked as an MCW demonstrator. This received Stevensons livery with Midland Classic fleet names. Relatively modern midibuses entering the fleet were Dennis Darts with bodywork by Carlyle, Wright and Plaxton as the company standardised on the Dart. These were later followed by longer, low-floor Dennis Dart SLFs with Plaxton Pointer bodywork which arrived from Trent Barton and Travel London, as well as a single Optare MetroRider. Larger heavyweight single-deckers began to appear too, including Wright Eclipse Urban-bodied Volvo B7Rs from various sources.

David Reeves, the owner of D&G Bus, and his fellow director Julian Peddle each obtained a 13% shareholding in the company in December 2009, joining James Boddice with 69% and John Mitchelson with 5%.

The first low-floor double-deckers arrived in 2010 when three Alexander ALX400-bodied Dennis Tridents arrived from Stagecoach London and Abellio London. Two more followed in 2011. They all received purpose-made sets of London-style blinds with Johnson lettering. They were later fitted with electronic displays. Originally dual-doored,

*Midland Classic only operated one Optare MetroRider, seen here in November 2009. It is in Birches Head working for RML Travel shortly before the company ceased trading in January 2010. The MetroRider was new to Shamrock Coaches of Pontypridd.*

*A Scania CN270UB OmniCity is seen at Uttoxeter after arriving on a 401 from Burton-on-Trent in March 2020. There are two of these stylish buses in the Midland Classic fleet, both of which were new to Reading Buses. They came to Midland Classic in 2018.*

*A Wright Solar-bodied Scania L94UB takes a break in Uttoxeter before departing on a 402A to Burton on Trent via Abbots Bromley in March 2020. This bus was new to Reading Transport.*

*One of 11 Wright Commander-bodied DAF SB220s acquired with the Arriva operations in Burton works a three to Winshill shortly after the takeover in September 2016. It is still in Arriva livery with Midland Classic fleet names.*

LEFT: *The London ADL Enviro400 is now the standard Midland Classic double-decker with ten ex-London examples in the fleet. One leaves Uttoxeter on a 401 for Burton-on-Trent in July 2019. It was new to First London and came via Tower Transit.*

they were later converted to single door. Another interesting acquisition was an East Lancs-bodied Dennis Falcon that came from Arriva Midlands but had been new to Midland Red North, ordered at a time when both Midland Red North and East Lancs were owned by Drawlane.

More modern heavy-duty single-deckers started arriving in 2011, this time Wright Solar-bodied Scania L94UBs from South Lancs Travel and Beestons of Hadleigh. These gradually made a start in replacing the Dennis Darts in the fleet.

The first Optare Solos entered the fleet in 2012 when two examples arrived from Felix of Stanley. Also acquired was an East Lancs Myllenium-bodied MAN 14.220 which, although repainted into fleet livery, did not stay in the fleet for too long.

More Wright Solar-bodied Scanias arrived in 2013, this time from South Lancs Travel. They entered service with their SLT select registrations but were later re-registered. The earlier Wright Eclipse-bodied Volvos were then sold to Diamond Bus. Later in the year an ADL Enviro300-bodied Scania K230UB demonstrator was trialled and was later purchased and re-registered from YN62 AAK to HK62 MCL -

indicating Midland Classic Limited.

A former London Buses Leyland Olympian part-open-topper also joined the fleet and was repainted into London red livery with a yellow band, like the surviving Routemaster.

The first brand-new buses purchased by the company were two 39-seat ADL Enviro200s which arrived in July 2014 with select registrations JB14 MCL and KW14 MCL. They were later joined by another Enviro200, a 9.6m 33-seater. This was a former Alexander Dennis demonstrator and like the Scania demonstrator before it was re-registered, from YY64 YKC to JB64 MCL. Also joining from South Lancs Travel was an Optare Olympus-bodied Scania N230UD.

In 2015 the first low-floor double-deckers in the fleet, five Dennis Tridents, were gradually replaced by younger ex-Arriva London Wright Pulsar Gemini-bodied DAF DB250s dating from 2003-04. Like the Tridents, these arrived as dual-door buses but were gradually converted to single-door. Joining these at around the same time were four ex-Transdev London Scania East Lancs OmniDekka double-deckers, along with a fifth former Go-Ahead London example. One of these was repainted into heritage Stevensons of Uttoxeter  yellow, white and black livery; it was also re-trimmed with the same blue and green seat moquette that was used on the large number of London Transport DMS Fleetlines that entered the Stevensons fleet from 1980.  An additional double-decker arriving at this time was Optare Spectra R2 NEG which was new to National Express Dundee and

*One of four brand-new Optare Metrocitys purchased to operate on former Arriva routes is running on service two to Edge Hill in September 2016. These buses are now being repainted into the new Airline 9 livery.*

ABOVE: *The sole Optare Olympus-bodied Scania N230UD in the fleet is seen in Burton-on-Trent in August 2016. It was new to South Lancs Travel of Atherton. Two similar vehicles arrived from Reading in 2018 but departed again after only a few months service.*

ABOVE: *Heritage liveries have featured on Midland Classic buses since the beginning, with the latest example being an ADL Enviro400 in the maroon and cream of the former Burton-on-Trent Corporation. It is working the 406 Uttoxeter Outer Circle service in July 2019. Burton Corporation buses never reached Uttoxeter.*

LEFT: *A unique bus in the Midland Classic fleet is this former demonstrator, an ADL Enviro300-bodied Scania K230UB seen here in Burton on Trent. This bus has since been re-registered with select registration HK62 MCL.*

had been the first low-floor double-decker to enter service in Scotland.

After ordering its first two brand-new buses from Alexander Dennis, the company changed direction in 2016 and turned to Optare for its next purchases, ordering two 10.1m-long Optare Metrocitys with 35 seats and USB charging points for its Lichfield local services 820 and 821.These entered service in April.

By now Midland Classic was operating a similar number of vehicles in Burton-on-Trent and Swadlincote as its main rival Arriva, so it came as no surprise when in April 2016 it was announced that Arriva Midlands had been in discussion with Midland Classic concerning the sale of Arriva's bus operations and depot in Wetmore Road, Burton-on-Trent. Not all the Arriva services in Burton would transfer. The X38 Derby to Burton service which was operated jointly with Trent Barton would stay with Arriva and be run from its Derby depot. And services from Burton to Coalville which extend to Leicester would transfer to the Arriva Coalville outstation. The deal was concluded, and the date of transfer was August 27, 2016. All remaining Arriva staff at Burton garage, along with 11 Wright-bodied DAF SB220s, transferred to Midland Classic under

TUPE - an acronym for the Transfer of Undertakings (Protection of Employment) Regulations 1981. The acquired buses received Midland Classic stickers applied over their Arriva livery; just one would receive full Midland Classic livery. The rest remained in Arriva livery until they were withdrawn.

The newly enlarged Midland Classic operation would see its peak vehicle requirement nearly double overnight from 24 to 46 as the former Arriva routes were integrated into the existing network. The main Uttoxeter to Burton via Tutbury and Hatton service was renumbered from 1 to 401 and the Uttoxeter Outer Circle service from 4 to 406, thereby reverting to their former Stevensons route numbers, as used before Arriva had taken over in 1994.

Four more brand-new Optare Metrocitys, this time 10.8m 39-seaters, were added to the fleet in September 2016 to work former Arriva routes, joining the two 35-seat 10.1m versions that had entered service earlier in the year.

Much more interesting was the arrival of an Alexander-bodied Leyland Olympian from Transdev Blazefield for the heritage fleet. This bus, F96 PRE, was one of a pair originally delivered new to Stevensons in 1988.

On December 31, 2016, the last day that non-low-floor buses could be used on normal bus services daily, Olympian F96 PRE joined Metrobus TOJ 592S and Routemaster RM 1168 for a swansong

ABOVE: *A Scania OmniDekka provides a glimpse of the past as it wears Stevensons of Uttoxeter heritage livery in Burton in September 2016. The TFA 13 registration was previously carried by a Stevensons Leyland Leopard coach and is owned by co-director Julian Peddle, who is a former Stevensons director. This bus was new to London Sovereign as YN54 OAG and has since reverted to its original number.*

RIGHT: *Before being replaced by a newer ADL Enviro400, a Wright Pulsar Gemini-bodied DAF DB250 loads in Burton for Clay Mills in 2016. It was new to Arriva London.*

ABOVE: *A Wright Solar-bodied Scania L94UB is seen in Burton-on-Trent on the X12 Flyer to Sutton Coldfield in August 2016. This route has now been cut back to Lichfield. The bus was new in 2005 to South Lancs Travel of Atherton.*

on route 21, Burton to Swadlincote. From now on appearances of these step-entrance buses on normal services would be limited to a few days each year.

Single-deckers arriving in 2017 were ADL Enviro200s from London operators Metroline and Tower Transit. The Tower Transit examples retained their dual-door layout because they lacked an offside emergency door. The arrival of these buses would lead to the withdrawal of the first of the Wright Commander-bodied DAF SB220s inherited from Arriva with the purchase of its Burton operations.

After running operations from two depots in Burton-on-Trent for eight months, the depot at Stanton Road finally shut on April 22, 2017, with all vehicles being based at the former Arriva depot at Wetmore Road.

A seasonal contract gained in the autumn was to provide transport for workers to the large Boots distribution warehouse at the Centrum 100 business park in Burton. This involved bringing workers in from Derby as the X39 service and from Nottingham as the X40. In later years additional contract workers would be brought in from more distant locations such as Birmingham and Newcastle-under-Lyme.

More double-deckers arrived in early 2018, with two Scania OmniDekkas coming from Reading to replace two East Lancs Olympus-bodied Scanias from the same source that had a very short working life at Midland Classic.

The same year also saw the company take on regular rail-replacement work to add to its portfolio of operations. This would take Midland Classic buses out of their traditional area to such places as Stourbridge, Rugby, Coventry, and Birmingham working for London Northwestern Railway.

Newer double-deckers arriving at the end of the year were seven ADL Enviro400s from Tower Transit but new to First London. The arrival of these would see a start to the withdrawal of the Wright Pulsar Gemini-bodied DAF DB250s.

Instead of receiving fleet livery, one of these Enviro400s received the heritage livery of Burton-on-Trent Corporation maroon and cream, complete with the corporation coat of arms. This livery had not been seen on buses in Burton since the mid-1970s when Burton-on-Trent Corporation was replaced by the new East Staffordshire District Council in the 1974 local government reorganisation. ESDC later introduced a new red, white and green livery for its buses.

The Optare Solo made a reappearance in the fleet when two arrived from Centrebus. They received fleet livery and branding for route two.

An interesting demonstrator in early 2019 was a

*ADL Enviro200 JB64 MCL seen here in Burton in August 2016 on a 22 to Swadlincote, was originally a demonstrator registered YY64 YKC. It was only 12 months old when purchased in 2015.*

Mercedes-Benz Sprinter with 26-seat Mellor Strata body. It was evaluated on several routes to test its suitability in service.

Having previously been engaged to design publicity material and timetables for the company, in 2019 Best Impressions, run by Ray Stenning, was commissioned to design a new livery for the X12 from Burton to Lichfield, and its stunning red, yellow and black X12 Flyer livery featuring more yellow was applied to two ADL Enviro200s.

An indication of the standard of service provided by Midland Classic for its customers was evident in March 2019 when it was judged to be the third-best operator in the United Kingdom by the independent Transport Focus survey for overall journey satisfaction. The following month saw the introduction of the Staffordshire County Council-sponsored 'Knot' ticket, to encourage people to use buses. This allowed a day's travel on buses across the whole of Staffordshire for £7, valid on any bus, at any time and on any day. Bus operators participating

alongside Midland Classic were Arriva Midlands, First Potteries, D&G Bus, Select Bus Services, Diamond and National Express West Midlands.

Three more former London Enviro400s arrived in September, this time from Metroline, along with three youthful Enviro200s from the recently closed fleet of Your Bus of Heanor, which became the youngest members of the fleet. All entered service in their former operators' liveries with Midland Classic fleet names before receiving a repaint into fleet livery.

October saw the introduction of new route Airline 9 by extending existing route nine between Burton and Ashby-de-la-Zouch to East Midlands Airport, offering an all-day service, seven days a week. Three of the Optare Metrocitys received branding for the Airline 9. Later these would start to be repainted into the livery with more yellow, like the Enviro200s on the X12.

Also reappearing in Stevensons livery for the first time in many years was heritage fleet member Leyland Olympian F96 PRE. It regained its original destination layout at the same time.

Over the last 15 years Midland Classic has expanded from an initial two buses to today's fleet of 57, in the process becoming the main operator in Burton-on-Trent, Swadlincote, Ashby, Uttoxeter, and Lichfield. Its first vehicles were interesting older buses with a link to the past, whereas today's fleet is modern and low floor with a strong London presence looking towards the future. The Enviro200 and Enviro400 are now the standard vehicles alongside a handful of Optare Metrocitys and some older Wright-bodied DAFs, with a sprinkling of others to add a bit of interest. One vehicle which has survived the test of time is Routemaster RM1168 which has been silently observing all the changes since the beginning.

*This ADL Enviro200 was the first new bus purchased by Midland Classic, in 2014. In 2019 it was repainted in this dedicated livery for the X12 service between Burton-on-Trent and Lichfield. Because of reductions to the X12 during the coronavirus pandemic it makes an appearance in Uttoxeter on a 401 to Burton in May 2020.*

*At first glance this Birkenhead Transport ADL might look like just another Enviro200 – but look more closely and you will see that it has three axles. This is because New Zealand has lower axle weight limits than most other countries where Enviro200s operate. New in 2018, this bus is a two-door 45-seater, one of 23 similar vehicles.*

In 2019 **Tim Carter** fulfilled a long-held ambition to visit New Zealand and was pleasantly surprised by the number of British-built buses he encountered.

# Brits abroad 3
## New and used in New Zealand

*Birkenhead Transport operates ADL single- and double-deckers. Here an Enviro500 heads north out of Auckland in the evening rush hour. The bus behind is a BCI operated by Ritchies Transport. AT Metro is a trading name for Auckland Transport, the body responsible not just for public transport but also roads, footpaths, parking, and cycling.*

ABOVE: *Most services in Auckland are operated by buses in AT Metro colours but there are exceptions including the central area InnerLink which uses a bright green livery. This ADL Enviro200 is operated by NZ Bus, successors to the one-time Stagecoach operation in the city.*

BELOW: *Bus Travel NZ operates three Wright StreetLite DF models. They were new in 2017 and are used on The Yellow Bus service linking Auckland Airport with nearby hotels and car and motorhome rental agencies. They were the first Wrightbus vehicles to be sold in New Zealand.*

*Ritchies Transport operates throughout New Zealand. This is Dunedin with an Optare Excel. The company bought 33 second-hand Excels in the mid-2000s, many of them coming from Reading Buses.*

*Tranzit Group ordered 114 Optare MetroCitys when it won contracts to provide many of the bus services in Wellington, New Zealand's capital. They were delivered in 2018. This one is in the colours of Metlink, the Greater Wellington regional transport authority. Tranzit was the biggest buyer of the MetroCity.*

ABOVE: *Rather different vehicles with a British connection in the Ritchies fleet are Scania K440s with Plaxton Elite bodies. Thirteen were supplied in 2017-18.*

RIGHT: *This MCV-bodied MAN14.240 is a former British bus in the Tranzit fleet. It was new to Diamond Bus in 2010 and was bought by Tranzit in 2013. Tranzit has 37 such vehicles bought second-hand from the UK.*

*Ritchies also operates local Baybus services in Rotorua with bilingual branding – cityride and, in Maori, eke-taone. The services are supported by the delightfully named Bay of Plenty Regional Council and the fleet includes such unusual vehicles as this Plaxton Primo, one of eight supplied in 2009 to Go-Bus of Hamilton, another city on North Island.*

# DOIG'S
## of Glasgow

Doig's of Glasgow was established in its present form at the start of the 1990s. **Billy Nicol** illustrates some of the varied types it has operated.

*Over the years Doig's has invested heavily in new vehicles. One of the first, in 1998, was this compact MAN 11.220 with 33-seat Berkhof Axial body.*

ABOVE: *The company's first new double-decker was delivered in 2005, an East Lancs-bodied Scania Omnidekka. It was the first low-floor double-decker for a Scottish independent.*

ALL PHOTOGRAPHS BY THE AUTHOR.

ABOVE: *The biggest double-decker operated by Doig's is this 100-seat three-axle Volvo. New in 2010, it is a B9TL with Optare Olympus body.*

LEFT: *A novel purchase in 2001 was this Scania L94UA with Wright Solar Fusion body. Very few small operators bought new articulated buses. Doig's used this one primarily on a shuttle service for the University of Strathclyde.*

LEFT: *A silver livery was adopted in the early 2000s and an early delivery in the new colours was this 2004 VDL SB4000 with Marcopolo Viaggio 350 body.*

*Doig's also buys Volvo coaches. Among those purchased in 2015 were a B8R with 70-seat Plaxton Leopard bodywork (LEFT) and a B11R with Spanish Sunsundegui bodywork (RIGHT).*

*The most recent double-decker, new in 2018, is an 86-seat ADL Enviro400 MMC seen at the Glasgow Science Centre. It replaced the 100-seat Volvo B9TL.*

*The company also runs small coaches. This is a Mercedes-Benz Vario O816D with Irmaos Mota bodywork. These are manufactured in Portugal and sold in the UK as the Turas. Unusually, this is a second-hand acquisition. The coach was new in 2013 to Smith of Gravesend and was bought by Doig's in 2014.*

*Both Scanias and Volvos were purchased new in 2019, the latter having Sunsundegui bodies. Two were 10.3m-long SC5 37-seaters based on the B8R chassis with Volvo's 7.7-litre engine.*

*A new type purchased in 2016 was this tri-axle Scania Higer Touring HD. The 13.7m-long coach is produced in China and has a Scania K410EB underframe. High-specification coaches such as this carry Platinum branding.*

# COLOURFUL
# Northern Ireland

Northern Ireland's bus and coach services are still largely provided by a public sector operator. But there is plenty of colour, as **Paul Savage** illustrates.

That part of the United Kingdom which is the six counties forming Northern Ireland (FATLAD as I was taught at school – Fermanagh, Armagh, Tyrone, Londonderry, Antrim, Down) covers an area of 5,460 square miles and has a population of almost 1.9 million. Its capital, on the east coast, is the still-busy port of Belfast (from the Irish Béal Feirste - mouth of the sandbank ford), which has about 342,000 residents though nearly twice that number in the metropolitan area.

*Belfast's east-west bus rapid transport system, Glider, replaced most Metro buses on corridors four and ten from September 2018. It is operated by Citybus with 32 Van Hool ExquiCity hybrid articulated buses, numbered 3200-31. Fleet number 3230 (OGZ 2230), here passing through Cromac Square on a westbound G1, is one of two additional vehicles ordered in May 2018 to boost capacity. It entered service in September 2019. The buses are 18m long with 42 seats and space for up to 58 standees.*

The biggest event in Northern Ireland in 2019 was the 148th open golf championship, hosted in July at Royal Portrush, on the north Antrim coast. A major transport operation was mounted with additional bus, coach, and train services, as well as park-and-ride from several sites. For the benefit of train passengers travelling from the Londonderry direction, a rail replacement service was provided between Coleraine and Portrush. Wright StreetDeck HEV 5000 (MXZ 6200), transferred north from the Metro operation in Belfast especially for the occasion, was one of the regular vehicles. It was the first hybrid bus in the fleet.

The golf championship saw Ulsterbus vehicles drafted into Coleraine depot from across the province, including Volvo B9TL/Wright Eclipse Gemini 2256 (OEZ 7256) from the Foyle Metro city services allocation at Londonderry. Buses allocated to Foyle Metro wear a livery of all-over burnt orange. Here 2256 is seen on park-and-ride duty at Portrush.

The scenic north Antrim coast is home to one of Northern Ireland's big tourist attractions, the Giant's Causeway. Ulsterbus services 402 and seasonal variation 402a serve the coastal route between Ballycastle and Coleraine, providing a useful link for locals and visitors alike. Frequencies have been much improved over the past few years, with hourly departures even in the depths of winter. In May 2019, Scania L94UB/Wright Solar 761 (TCZ 1761), new in 2003, departs the Causeway stop on the 402a variant en route to Bushmills Distillery, Portrush and Coleraine.

About 75 miles to the northwest is the second city, officially Londonderry, but Derry to many and most of its residents. The population there is about 93,500 in the urban area. The city is also known as the Maiden City as its walls have never been breached despite being besieged on three occasions, the most significant being the Siege of Derry in 1688-89.

Armagh, to the south of Belfast is the ecclesiastical capital of the island of Ireland, being the seats of the Archbishop of Armagh (Anglican) and the Primate of All Ireland (Roman Catholic). In between these three cities is Lough Neagh, the largest lake in the British Isles with a surface area of 151 square miles; by comparison Windermere, the largest lake in England, covers less than six square miles.

Northern Ireland is the only part of the United Kingdom apart from London where bus services have not been deregulated. Most services are provided by the state-owned Citybus (branded Metro) in Belfast and Ulsterbus beyond, including its Goldline express services network. The busy Goldline 212 route between Belfast and Londonderry runs every 15 minutes at peak hours, with the first journey leaving Derry at 04:15 and the last from Belfast at 01:00.

*The bus service between the visitor centre and the Giant's Causeway proper is provided by Ulsterbus, usually with two buses from a fleet of four in this green livery. One of two Optare Solo M925SRs is 1935 (TFZ 9935), shown here returning from the causeway along the single-track road. The other two vehicles operating the service are a Plaxton Primo and an Optare Solo M850SL.*

Belfast and Dublin Airport, about 100 miles south, are linked by Ulsterbus/Bus Éireann routes X1 and X2a, plus Aircoach 705X, which is operated by First Northern Ireland; Aircoach services in Ireland are operated by Last Passive, another FirstGroup company. The Belfast-based First Northern Ireland fleet consists of seven Volvo B11R/Plaxton Panther 3 coaches new in February 2018. IGZ 6131 is numbered F35 locally, 20935 nationally, and was photographed arriving at the Glengall Street departure point.

Translink's Great Victoria Street depot in Belfast has an allocation of eight 63-seat Volvo B11RTs with Sunsundegui SC5 bodies for its share of the Dublin service. There are 30 coaches in this batch, delivered in 2019. Photographed from the Boyne Bridge overlooking Belfast's Europa Bus Centre, 1124 (XUI 2924) departs for Dublin Airport and city centre on the X2a service, a journey of about two hours and 20 minutes.

As the biggest operator in Northern Ireland, Ulsterbus maintains a fleet of luxury coaches for private hire and its luxury tours programme, which covers the British Isles and continental Europe. One such vehicle is 128 (BXI 328) a Scania K420 with 52-seat Irizar PB body. It was new in May 2009 and registered with a number transferred from an Optare Solo, but originally used on one of the final delivery of Leyland Leopards. Having been delivered in white, with stripes in green and two shades of blue, it now wears the latest version of Ulsterbus Tours livery with the stripes in three shades of blue. It is seen here in Belfast's Donegal Square North.

The Goldline network of Ulsterbus express services links Belfast with towns and cities across Northern Ireland using a fleet of, mostly, Scania coaches, including two batches of Scania K410s with Caetano Invictus double-deck coachwork. The first 12, delivered in 2016, were 13.2m-long 76-seaters, the next 12 in 2017-18 were even longer at 14.3m with 86 seats. Fleet number 2038 (IXZ 1838), from the first batch, was photographed in Belfast's High Street in April 2019, when it was allocated to Coleraine for route 218 which linked Coleraine and Belfast. It has since moved to Londonderry and been replaced by a Volvo B11RT/ Sunsundegui SC5.

Many visitors to Belfast come to learn about RMS Titanic and the disaster which befell it, the Titanic Experience in the city's famous shipyard area being a huge draw. Having set down its passengers, a Jonckheere-bodied Volvo B11R from the fleet of Bernard Kavanagh of Urlingford, Co Tipperary, heads past the large metal Titanic lettering on its way to the coach parking area.

Just to prove that the weather in Northern Ireland isn't always dry, Ulsterbus Optare Solo M850SL1925 (XEZ 3356), from the Bangor allocation, is seen here on a rainy day in October 2019 at the North Down town of Donaghadee - just 22 miles across the North Channel from Scotland's Rhinns of Galloway. Fleet number 1925 had just arrived from Bangor, six miles west along the coast.

Rural services provided by Ulsterbus are relatively frequent compared with many parts of Great Britain, though often operate either between or around school times. Belfast also has its Citybus-operated Glider, the cross-city bus rapid transit service, which uses a fleet of purple-liveried Van Hool ExquiCity bendy-buses. Rail services are provided by Northern Ireland Railways, with all three companies operating under the Translink banner, intended to suggest integration of service.

Today it is by some margin the largest public sector bus operator in the UK, with nearly 1,100 buses, express service and touring coaches providing 300 routes from 20 principal depots across Northern Ireland. The sister Metro business in Belfast has another 275 vehicles.

Some cross-border routes are joint with Bus Éireann or Irish Rail, though both Bus Éireann and Ulsterbus also operate cross-border routes. For example, Bus Éireann routes 64/480 reach Derry from Sligo and beyond while Ulsterbus route 70 provides the link between Armagh and Monaghan. Services between Dundalk and Newry are operated by Bus Éireann, with a competing, more direct service from the long-established Halpenny Transport, Blackrock, which celebrated its centenary in 2020.

As the accompanying images show, there is a lot of variety to be found in Northern Ireland's bus and coach operations.

*Northern Ireland's second city is Londonderry (officially) or Derry (as it is more widely called). In 2014, Her Majesty's Revenue and Customs acted against the Londonderry and Lough Swilly Railway Company, which went into liquidation and ran its last services on April 19. It had served the people of Derry and northwest Co Donegal since 1863; it had not run a train, though, since 1953. The Swilly's first bus route, in 1929, linked Derry and the seaside town of Buncrana and it still did so in 2014. On closure, the National Transport Authority granted a temporary licence to operate the route to McGonagle of Buncrana, which still runs it today using a pair of former Webberbus of Bridgwater Optare Versas and this ex-Courtney, Bracknell, Optare Solo M920SL.*

*A Bus Éireann Wright StreetLite DF is seen in Newry in the blue-based National Transport Authority livery. It has come from Dundalk on route 160 via Ravensdale. The National Transport Authority has supplied 88 StreetLites to Bus Éireann, Go-Ahead Ireland and City Direct to improve town and city services across the country; this one has obviously strayed from its intended duties.*

# Get your kicks
# on Route 26

**Chris Drew** tracks an Isle of Wight bus route.

Memories of my first Isle of Wight holiday have been dimmed by the years but there are moments of trials and tribulations that have hung on in my brain. The family crammed into one long seat on the top deck of a bus. Then there was the time my dear old dad's false teeth made a bid for freedom on a particularly bumpy ride. There was smoke that would emanate from the bottom of the garden of the cottage we stayed at. Truth be told, I was only five years old and the beach, the paddle boats on a lake nearby and a large model of the Isle of Wight on the sea-front at Ventnor held almost all my attention.

Later I was to find out the bench seating was of a type fitted to what was called a 'lowbridge' bus and that my dad needed a better denture fixative. The smoke that curled and hung in the bushes like a ghostly apparition at the end of the garden came from the steam trains arriving or leaving Ventnor station through a tunnel which ran under our holiday home. I was never to see those trains in steam again and, indeed, Ventnor was left totally bereft of trains when the line from Shanklin was closed in 1966.

It was to be another ten years before the family was to holiday on the island again. Ventnor was the venue chosen once more. By then I had been

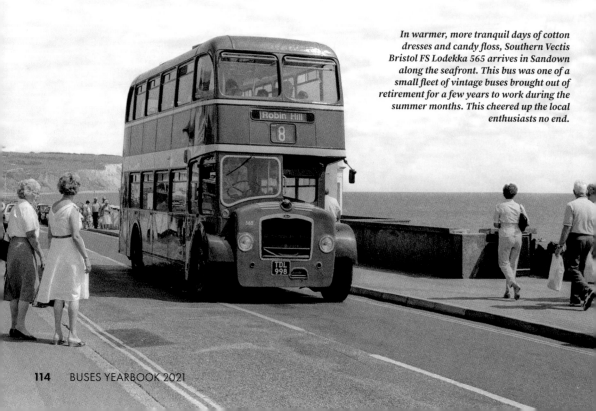

*In warmer, more tranquil days of cotton dresses and candy floss, Southern Vectis Bristol FS Lodekka 565 arrives in Sandown along the seafront. This bus was one of a small fleet of vintage buses brought out of retirement for a few years to work during the summer months. This cheered up the local enthusiasts no end.*

Many of the island fleet's older buses found retirement in Hope and Small Hope but in later years it was possible to travel on such as this unusual Bristol RELL with cut down ECW bodywork named Shanklin's Pony.

bitten by the bus bug and had found out what they were for ... and in quite a big way. I had purchased a camera which I could trust to do the job I wanted it to do and at the age of 15, my parents gave me room to do it in. They thought the island was a safe environment, safe enough for me to be let loose on the bus services and as a present they had bought me an island bus pass and timetable. This did not preclude me going on journeys with them, of course, but it did give me a choice in case we did not agree on the destination. It was not to be very long before I crossed paths with Southern Vectis bus route 26. It was going to take me to the wilder side of the island.

I must point out at this juncture that the photographs that accompany these words have been taken over the intervening years since, but along the course of the 26 as I found it in 1968.

The driver of this bus, open-top Lodekka OT5, held his nerve and crawled up Cowleaze Hill after which one could relax with heady views over Luccombe, the Chine and the English Channel beyond.

In my youth Ventnor bus station was a very rudimentary affair with off-road parking set at various angles. One-time coach 1952 Bristol LS6G 857 emphasises the less than flat nature of the village.

The route 26 I became acquainted with that year began its journey in Sandown. This was a place that fancied itself as a real seaside holiday resort with wide, shallow sandy beaches. Those same beaches had proved to be too much of a temptation to foreign armies in previous times. The French invaded in 1545 and later again in the 18th century by which time several forts had been strategically placed to repel these skirmishers. The Victorian age saw the railway reach the village and as with many others that saw a connection to the outside world in this way, it rapidly grew to be the town it is today.

There was another war that was to leave its mark upon Sandown. As part of the D-Day offensive towards the latter half of the World War Two, Sandown was used as a pumping station, sending oil along PLUTO, the Pipe Line Under The Ocean to the beachheads on the French coast. To this end,

the local ice cream factory and the golf course were adapted to camouflage the pumping equipment.

The 26 followed the ribbon of housing, through the village of Lake, crossing the railway twice before encountering the old-world charm of Shanklin. Leaving the bus at the Old Town with its genteel tea shops with their thatched roofs, it was a quiet stroll down to the beaches of Hope and Small Hope where one could ride upon the open-top buses.

As well as being home to a procession of older buses, Shanklin is also where Charles Darwin wrote his thesis on the On the Origin of Species! It took him 18 months to write and one must wonder how many answers to the many questions he found in Shanklin.

The serious work of Route 26 started on leaving Shanklin. The route encountered its first obstacle, the stiff climb up Cowleaze Hill. It was not usual for a driver to work his way down through the gearbox until the inevitable crunch followed the rapid application of the hand brake. With first gear safely acquired, forward momentum was regained with much blue smoke, oily smells, juddering and grinding noises. To many, but not all, this was thought of as thrilling.

As you crest Cowleaze Hill, the far view is of Dunnose Head, a high and imposing geological feature that has been used as a triangulation point in mapping for many years. It is also the place of many a shipwreck. From there the route tumbles off St Boniface Down and into the natural amphitheatre that is Ventnor.

Ventnor is a place with precious little level walking. It has almost a Mediterranean feel about it. It is thought of as an exclusive resort and, indeed, it was once called Mayfair-by-the-Sea because of the wealthy Londoners who would spend the summer there. The town elders were quick to exploit this and erected a pier at which steamers could call. There were soon services from Littlehampton which connected with fast trains from London. Other steamers called in from Southsea, Bournemouth and served other piers already situated on the island. By 1866 the railway reached Ventnor with up to 20 journeys a day. One of the services was a non-stop train called The Invalid Express for consumptive patients to take the sea air.

Like the rest of the island during the World

*Early Bristol K5G 703 appeared to have had a run-in with a tree. You can just make out a couple of people on the top deck attempting to clear the debris.*

War Two, Ventnor was put at the front line of the country's defences. A huge radar station was erected on St Boniface Down to give as much warning as possible of an imminent attack. This meant that the town was considered a legitimate target and was attacked by the Luftwaffe on several occasions leaving 120 buildings destroyed with 16 fatalities.

After leaving Ventnor the 26 moved inland to Whitwell, famous for its strange red cast iron water outlets in the streets known as lions or red boys.

*At the time this photograph of Bristol FLF 617 was taken in 1968, the original road to Blackgang Chine was still in use as seen by the Bristol LD in the distance. However, as with the rest of the southwest-facing coast on the island, erosion put paid to that about 20 years ago and a new road and junction was built further inland to regain access to the chine.*

These were put in as an act of great generosity by two local landowners in the late 19th Century when the water in the village began to cause illness amongst the villagers. On one of my motorbike excursions in later years, I had a lucky find on the road into Whitwell, one of the island's oldest open-top buses in winter plumage. An early Bristol K5G 703 painted in all-over Tilling green with NBC lettering looked as though it had had a run in with a tree and had a load of branches filling the top deck. This and a sister bus are well known by enthusiasts as being some of the oldest buses in the UK still with their original owner. A short way further down the road is the village of Niton, famous for its hostelries, well known to participants of the Beer and Buses weekend.

Here the 26 regained the coast road and a long crawl ensued over St Catherine's Down on the way to Blackgang Chine. It was on a fast journey downhill in the other direction that the structural integrity of my father's false teeth failed, much to the rest of the family's amusement. Here at Blackgang Chine one could see many of the island's coach owners' vehicles ticking as they cooled down from their morning exertions. It was a Mecca on the Island Tour. Even mystery tours would drop off wide-eyed children while their parents stood checking their pockets for change to cope with the expenses to follow. It has always struck me that there is something odd about a mystery tour on the Isle of Wight. It is no mystery unless you see fish passing the windows! Close by there were two lighthouses to visit, St Catherine's Point on the southern-most edge of the island and St Catherine's Oratory, better known as the Pepper Pot, which is set several hundred feet higher on the downs. Built in 1314 it is a 35ft-tall octagonal shell which was manned for centuries by priests trying to prevent shipwrecks.

Looking past the distant LD in the image of the coast road at Blackgang Chine on the previous page, the road became Blythe Shute which dropped down to St Andrew's Church at Chale. The 14th century building has a ring of six bells with one of them dating from about 1360. There are also a set of fine stained-glass windows from the hands of Charles Eamer Kempe.

At this point, it may be good to give a little history

*Not that you can see much in the fog, but this Dennis Dart 308 is darting through Chale. In a previous life the Dart's BUF registration would have been more at home 50 miles east along the coast.*

This image is from a painting representing a member of the second batch of Aces acquired by Southern Vectis in 1936. It is set somewhere on the Military Road.

of the route. It began in the 1930s when work on a replacement road between Ventnor and Freshwater was started. The erosion of cliffs on the southwest coast meant that roads in the area were unsafe and, indeed, in some places disappeared into the sea! The new road was grandly titled the Military Road. As soon as possible Southern Vectis applied for a licence to operate a service which would start at Ryde. It called at Ryde airport then headed south to use the new road and end at Alum Bay. Although the road was not finished, a licence was granted in 1934 and until the final tarmac was laid, the route had to be diverted inland at Compton Farm. There was another problem: in places the new road was only nine feet wide so as part of the deal, it was stipulated the service was to be run by 20-seat buses. To this end a small fleet of Harrington-bodied Dennis Aces was acquired. Southern Vectis was already well versed with the manufacturer's products. The first six arrived in 1934 and were followed by two more in 1936.

There were several large buildings dotted around the island. One at Brook, about halfway along the Military Road, was said to have been put to a sinister use during the Second World War. In 1910 the foundations were laid for Brook Hill House. The owner, Sir Charles Seely, conceived of a large house with grand views of the island's sunsets. He built it at the top of the hill under advice from his doctor as he suffered from bronchial troubles. The irony is that he died very soon after it was finished in 1915. It was later found out by chance that the expanse of widows reflected the setting sun and were used as a landmark by the German air force on its way to bomb Portsmouth. It is thought that is why the house was never targeted on raids.

Compton Bay is just a mile or so further on from Brook and was the closest the road came to the clay cliffs at the low level. It is even closer now. Compton Bay nowadays is famous for surfing at high tide and a petrified forest at low. The two do not mix.

From Compton Bay the road climbed a long slog of a hill over Compton Down. The down is owned and managed by the National Trust and consists of 196.3 hectares which are designated a Site of Special Scientific Interest for both biological and geological features. It is also one of the most photogenic areas for the photography of the local transport. In one direction the views back along the coast to Blackgang are uninterrupted, while the scene looking towards Freshwater can provide the backdrop of Tennyson Down.

Freshwater was nearly the site of my undoing. It was often the case that the 26 heading for Yarmouth would wait to meet the 26 going in the other direction. The 27 to Newport was also timed to arrive about five minutes later. On one occasion I sat in horror as the 26 I was on heading west passed the 26 going east and as I arrived in the town the 27 was disappearing in a cloud of blue smoke. A quick check of the timetable told me a 28 was leaving in 15 minutes which, with luck, would connect with a 17 in Newport. This would deliver me back to Ventnor just in time for an evening meal. It worked but, it did push the boundary of being sensible a little.

After this point the 26 headed back east towards Yarmouth with views from the top deck of Hurst Castle on the north island. Yarmouth is situated on one of the two rivers on the Isle of Wight to be called the Yar. Properly called the Western Yar, it drains the marshes which spread inland and almost

cut it off from the rest of the island. These marshes protected the original inhabitants, the Belgae, from invasion until 43AD when like almost everywhere else, the Romans (of What did they ever do for us? fame) moved in and took over. Later Jutes, Saxons and Danes all took a turn at living on the island and, indeed, it was the Saxons who first gave the town its name, Ermud meaning muddy estuary. Sounds simple that; you could imagine a Saxon nobleman astride his horse, asking his minion what this was and him replying 'Ere's mud' and the name stuck...and so did the mud. Through the ages the name evolved. In the 13th century, it was called Yaremuthe (more akin to a mixer with gin) and carried on changing little by little until it finally arrived at today's spelling.

Today there is a large boating community that uses the marina and it is one of the gateways for entry on to the island. In 1860 a road bridge was built, and a toll levied for crossing it. The building of the bridge, a new breakwater, pier, and the arrival of the railway all in a few years, changed the character of the town completely. The bridge was a

*The house reportedly used as a landmark by the World War Two Luftwaffe is located on Brook Hill behind 1955 Lodekka 531 which had just passed the road junction to Brook Village.*

single-carriageway wooden structure which could be lifted to let small boats through. The toll was eventually scrapped in 1934 when the Isle of Wight Council bought the bridge, but it was not until 1987 that a new, much wider bridge was completed.

At the time of my holiday in 1968, the route was approximately 27 miles long and took just two hours to complete. On one day I counted six Lodekkas running the route, mostly LDs, but at least one FS appeared, and a brand-new FLF with a paper sticker on the window over the bonnet. The 26 was a summer-only service and because of its length, it was treated by many visitors to the island as an unofficial tour.

Just as an aside, under the Yar Bridge Act of 1856, vessels have a right of way over road traffic using the bridge. Although nowadays you must book in advance if you wish to have the bridge raised to let your boat through.

RIGHT: *Tennyson Down provides the backdrop for this 2012 ADL Enviro400 in Vectis Blue livery, the private hire side of the company.*

BELOW: *Southern Vectis has operated bus routes over the old and new bridges in Yarmouth for many years. A pair of Scanias was seen together crossing in 2014. This was a very lucky shot as going by the timetable this meeting should not happen.*

Photographs of buses tend, naturally enough, to focus on the vehicles. **Tony Wilson** suggests that there are often benefits in stepping back and setting the bus in the wider picture. All photographs by the author.

# BUSES

*During the 1970s era of the National Bus Company a few subsidiaries required small buses to fit through narrow streets and down country lanes, especially in more rural areas. During early 1972 Western National acquired six short 33-seat Marshall-bodied Bristol LHS6Ls, numbered 88-93 (VOD 88-93K). That they were known as the 'Vodkas' may be an apocryphal tale. Here fleet number 92 trundles out of Truro city centre in July 1978, passing between two different generations of Ford's best-selling Cortina.*

# IN THE SCENE

Apart from the Tinsley Viaduct of the M1 motorway in the background, there is little else that remains from this picture. The once famous Tinsley cooling towers were demolished many years ago in the usual spectacular fashion with explosive devices. Perhaps not so spectacular was what happened to the bus in the foreground. It started life as one of five East Lancs-bodied Leyland Atlantean double-deckers supplied to East Staffordshire District Council in 1978. It was acquired by Andrews Sheffield Omnibus in 1993, at which point the chassis was lengthened and fitted with a new East Lancs single-deck body. It is entering Meadowhall Interchange in August 1997.

The mills and high stone-built buildings of Sowerby Bridge in March 1998 overlook First Calderline 1659 (A659 KUM), a bus which had originally been part of the West Yorkshire PTE fleet. This green and cream livery dated back to Yorkshire Rider; the company created in 1986 to take over the PTE's bus operations. First Calderline covered the former Yorkshire Rider operations in Calderdale and Halifax, and 1659 from 1983 was one of 15 Duple Dominant dual-purpose Leyland Tigers.  All the buildings in the background still stand, but with different occupants.

One of First Group's Wright StreetDecks, 35149 (SN65 OMT), passes over the River Bure from Hoveton to Wroxham on its way to Norwich in May 2019. The bus was new in 2015 for First's Bristol fleet and moved to First Eastern Counties in 2018.

During 2014 two routes were incorporated into one as the X17 and linked Matlock in Derbyshire via Chesterfield to Sheffield in South Yorkshire. Operated by Stagecoach Yorkshire's Stonegravels depot in Chesterfield, five new Gold-specification Scania N230UDs with ADL Enviro400 bodywork were acquired and ran the service until July 2018. From then the route was extended north from Sheffield to Barnsley, and another new fleet of double-deckers took over. This time eight ADL Enviro400 MMCs, again to Gold specification. Fleet number 11124 (SK68 LUR) tackles one of many hills on the route in February 2019.

LEFT: *In late 1972 and early 1973 NBC subsidiary Maidstone & District acquired 20 Leyland Atlanteans with 78-seat MCW bodywork as fleet numbers 5701-5720 (FKM 701-720L). During 1981 two of the buses were reconfigured with 69 dual-purpose seats to serve on the 990-group of Medway Town commuter services. They were repainted all-over black, relieved by a red sash down either side and given Invictaway fleet names. The logo incorporates the White Horse of Kent. Here 5718 is heading across Vauxhall Bridge into central London to take up an evening journey on route 992 to Gillingham.*

RIGHT: *From a busy inner city to the tranquil surroundings of the North Nottinghamshire countryside. Long-established bus and coach operator Marshalls of Sutton-on-Trent has served the local community using a variety of vehicles in this pleasant blue and cream livery. This is illustrated well on DS51 (S4 YRR) a Plaxton Pointer-bodied Dennis Dart SLF as it departs its home location in October 2009, bound for Newark. In the background one of the once numerous mills is now converted into a dwelling.*

LEFT: *Over the years the revenue-earning lives of many London buses have been extended after their sale to other operators. One such company was Axe Valley Motor Transport based in Sidmouth, Devon, where former London Buses Leyland Olympian with ECW body C94 CHM heads out of the town on an early morning journey of route 899 to Seaton Sea Front. Originally a dual-door vehicle to cope with the South London crowds, by July 2011 it had been converted to single-door and received its new owner's colours as it sparkled in the summer sunshine.*

As the clock on Sheffield City's imposing town hall approaches two o'clock a couple of First South Yorkshire Wright StreetLite DF single-deckers pause at the bus stops on Pinstone Street alongside the Peace Gardens. Both buses were relatively new to the fleet, 63033 (SK63 LKH) ahead of 63129 (SN14 DVZ), as they waited time in April 2014, both on the high-frequency cross-city route 22. Clearly one was either late or the other early on this occasion.

RIGHT: *St George's Hall is a neoclassical venue for events and concerts in Liverpool, and it provides the backdrop for Liverline 615 (B155 TRN) in August 1996. Liverline was a deregulation-era independent which was acquired by British Bus and became part of that group's North Western subsidiary. This Leyland Olympian with ECW bodywork was one of eight supplied to the Ribble subsidiary of NBC in 1984.*

*The first couple of months of 2015 saw First Manchester take delivery of 20 Volvo B5LHs with Wright Gemini 3 bodies as fleet numbers 39237-39256. All in a purple-based livery, they were for new services V1 and V2 that linked the city centre with Leigh on the western side of Greater Manchester. Marketed as Vantage, the two routes utilised a guided busway, part of which was built on the alignment of an old railway line. This is 39248 (BL65 YZK), in April 2016. The elevated view from the upper deck of a similar bus affords a splendid view of the undulating nature of the busway.*

*A bustling city centre greets a McColl's of Dumbarton bus as it emerges from beneath the platforms and massive glass structure of Glasgow Central Station in September 2011. Fleet number 2060 (P498 BRS) was a Volvo B6LE with Alexander ALX200 bodywork which had been new to Stagecoach Bluebird in 1996.*

LEFT: *A new Myllennium for the Millennium at the Millennium Dome. April 2000 and a time for bright new beginnings including a fleet of 17 DAF SB220 East Lancs Myllennium-bodied single-deckers for London Central. The buses were for new routes M1 and M2 serving North Greenwich. MD1 (V1 GMT) with the Dome behind, departs on the M2 to the railway station at Greenwich. The Dome lives on as the O2 Arena and regularly hosts concerts and other live events.*

RIGHT: *When Stagecoach withdrew its Coasthopper services it could have led to a major loss of connections along the North Norfolk coastal roads. However, two operators stepped in. One of these was Sanders Coaches of Holt, which kept the Coasthopper name. For this the company acquired ten surplus Wright-bodied Volvo B7RLEs from Go-Ahead South Coast. The buses retained their previous More livery, upon which Sanders placed its own branding. The big skies and open spaces along the A149 coast road in June 2019 provide the surroundings for 504 (HF54 HFP), as it passes through the pretty village of Salthouse.*

*With buses shown from the past five decades it is back to 1970 for the final picture. Most buses finish their days in a scrapyard. Two once handsome Bristols are illustrated at Junction 4 on the M1 motorway near Edgware, a double-deck K and single-deck LS both with ECW bodies, and thought to be from the Hants & Dorset company. Both were on suspended tow bound for the Barnsley scrapyards and the end of their days, as they journeyed north during the late afternoon with minimal traffic around. This part of the M1 had been open for four years, from 1966, and was of a concrete construction.*